Breaking Free

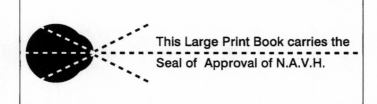

This Large Print Book carries the
Seal of Approval of N.A.V.H.

Breaking Free

Frank Freed, Ph.D.

Thorndike Press • Waterville, Maine

Published in 2006 by arrangement with Guideposts a Church Corporation.

Thorndike Press® Large Print Christian Living.

The tree indicium is a trademark of Thorndike Press.

The text of this Large Print edition is unabridged.
Other aspects of the book may vary from the original edition.

Set in 18 pt. Plantin by Carleen Stearns.

Printed in the United States on permanent paper.

Library of Congress Cataloging-in-Publication Data
Freed, Frank, 1922–
    [Breaking free when you're feeling trapped]
    Breaking free / by Frank Freed.
      p. cm.
    Originally published: Breaking free when you're feeling trapped. Wheaton, Ill. : H. Shaw Publishers, c1997.
    ISBN 0-7862-8625-3 (lg. print : hc : alk. paper)
    1. Self-actualization (Psychology) — Religious aspects — Christianity.   2. Christian life.   I. Title.
BV4598.2.F75 2006
248.8´6—dc22   2006005786

Breaking Free

As the Founder/CEO of NAVH, the only national health agency solely devoted to those who, although not totally blind, have an eye disease which could lead to serious visual impairment, I am pleased to recognize Thorndike Press★ as one of the leading publishers in the large print field.

Founded in 1954 in San Francisco to prepare large print textbooks for partially seeing children, NAVH became the pioneer and standard setting agency in the preparation of large type.

Today, those publishers who meet our standards carry the prestigious "Seal of Approval" indicating high quality large print. We are delighted that Thorndike Press is one of the publishers whose titles meet these standards. We are also pleased to recognize the significant contribution Thorndike Press is making in this important and growing field.

Lorraine H. Marchi, L.H.D.
Founder/CEO
NAVH

★ Thorndike Press encompasses the following imprints: Thorndike, Wheeler, Walker and Large Print Press.

Contents

Acknowledgments

I wish to acknowledge the patience of my loving wife Evelyn, who "out-deferred" me in the writing of this book.

My writing mentor Robert C. Larson taught me how to translate the spoken word into the written word. Bob has been a great friend as well as a gifted teacher.

When once I wondered if the book could be completed on schedule, motivation flowed from my editor Joan Guest, who just said, "Sure!" Thank you, Joan.

Trapped . . .

I feel trapped in all the choices
I wish I hadn't made,
Still trapped in painful past
events
Where I too long have stayed
I feel trapped in fear of all
the things
That never came to be,
And trapped in angry feelings
I allowed to savage me.
I feel trapped in frantic pairings
With secrets I won't share,
Still trapped with dark and
gloomy thoughts
Which lead me to despair
I feel trapped, up until now . . .
By all the things above
But now believe that my way out
Is to speak the truth with love.

Introduction to This Edition

Dr. Frank Freed is one of the extraordinary people of our time. His compassion for those who are hurting and his keen desire to help them break free from painful difficulties into a meaningful healing and gain release have, I believe, been the main impetus of his life.

Frank Freed has had a wonderful career as an esteemed psychologist in the southern California area. Through personal life experiences, as well as in the private counseling room, he is able to talk to the pain life can bring to us all at one time or another.

When my husband, Norman Vincent Peale, and I first came to New York City in 1932 during the Great

Depression, he was inundated with requests for pastoral counseling, and he saw and listened to every troubled person who came. Human problems are always with us, but at that time they were accentuated by the fear, hopelessness, and despair caused by the Depression.

Norman felt ill prepared for the problems posed in these sessions, having only scanty training in psychology. He cared and listened patiently and then began to be suspicious that deeper problems often lay beneath the patient's assumptions about his or her problem. Deciding that he needed help and professional understanding he eventually was led to join in counseling people with a gifted psychiatrist. This was very, very rare for its time and many were skeptical, but it has led to the wonderful gift of many caring, spiritual counselors, including Dr. Frank Freed, who care about and want to help those who are in need.

In particular, Frank's book, *Breaking Free*, discusses the choices — positive and negative — that each person may make to either conquer or be conquered by life. The choices we make daily in relationships, in business, in school, in our finances, whatever problems faced, can be approached in such a way as to fully realize the power of decision. "Will I be gripped by fear?" or "Will I choose to walk through the fear to faith?" Another: "Will I be haunted by painful experiences of my past?" or "Will I choose to become better — instead of bitter?" Relating to this question,

Frank himself tells in a very sensitive way of his own loss during World War II and his choosing to become "better" and not "bitter."

I gained an increase of knowledge and insight into life's problems by reading *Breaking Free*. You will discover the "eight words that matter." I encourage you, as does the author, that you bring these words that are especially positive closer into your daily vocabulary.

As you study *Breaking Free*, I would encourage you to look for those key phrases that spark something special in your thoughts. Frank Freed calls them "phrases of truth," and he suggests writing the day's date in the margin and whispering a prayer, "Thank you, Lord."

I am thankful Frank Freed has put

together these insightful thoughts for our benefit. May you be blessed by his writing.

Ruth Stafford Peale
Chairman Emeritus,
Guideposts

Introduction

Every day, millions of Americans seek counsel from a pastor, priest, rabbi or talk-show host on radio or television. What are they looking for? What answers have not been found in their lives? And why do they keep on asking, and probing, and putting themselves on the line in their quest for answers that make sense?

The answer lies in the title of the second book of the Bible: Exodus, the story of a people looking for a way out. People who have come to me for counseling for the past several decades have one primary obstacle in their lives: They feel trapped and they desperately want a way out. They feel boxed in, suffocated by life and its challenges. They feel they can neither stay in nor get out of relationships and situations that are destroying them physically, emotionally and spiritually. They watch their daily soap operas, hoping they'll find temporary relief as they mesh their own life's struggles into the roller-coaster emotions of their favorite TV personality. But it is only that: temporary. For a fleeting moment, at least, the viewers feel they are not alone in their pain. In a land of freedom, they continue to choose bondage for themselves, hoping against hope that what television promises will be the long-sought elixir for their pain and despair.

In the preceding paragraph, one word appears several times. This word is *feel*. Not long ago we held the mistaken notion that we had little or no control over the way we felt. It was just natural to feel a certain way, we believed, so we conditioned ourselves to let our dominant feelings rule our lives.

A New Way of Thinking

We now know better. Today we have undeniable clinical evidence that we *create* our feelings by the way we choose to think. Preceding every feeling is a thought that calls it into existence. If we accept this as fact, then it must follow as night follows day that *the way out of a feeling comes with the changing of our minds and the way we think.*

Since the beginning of time, men and women from every culture at one time or another have felt the grass was greener on the other side of the fence. Surely there would be better economic opportunities, better relationships, better health, better amusements, better everything . . . *if I could just get over there where the grass is so much greener.* So, like the Prodigal Son in the New Testament, those seekers of a better life chose to leave everything behind to luxuriate in the new, greener turf that would surely make their lives better and their fondest dreams come true. The one thing they did not take into account was that *they were taking themselves with them* — a fact that, in itself, could change the color of the newly visited grass. The sudden awareness? The grass was not greener after all. Instead, they quickly learned, it was only green for those who chose to water it, fertilize it, and treat it with tender, loving care.

It's All about Choices

The quality of our lives always has been determined by the choices you and I have made. Not surprisingly, the riches or poverty that will define our lives in the days ahead also will depend on our choices today. And those choices will depend on our thinking. The Proverbs tell us that as a person thinks in his heart, so is he — or she. A new kind of thinking can get us out of life's traps as we make the exodus from the defective and ineffective thoughts of our past.

Max DePree, a recognized authority on leadership abilities, points out just how changed thinking works. He writes in *Leadership Jazz* that many people think a promotion at work indicates they are already competent in the new area. He suggests a change in thinking to recognize that what a promotion really means is, "Good grief, have I got a lot to learn!" DePree says that we get into a trap when we erroneously believe that things are the way we want them to be. We get out of the trap by facing our reality and thinking about the way things really are.

A final word before we get started. When we feel trapped, it's usually because we have not understood this one key element in our thinking process: It's always easier to get into something than to get out of it. I've never found anyone with a satisfactory argument against this life principle. This could refer to a relationship, a business association, a course of study, a financial deal, you name it. Link this in your mind with the truth that we are all free up to the point of choice, after which the choice has the power to control the chooser.

The very fact that you have chosen to read this book would indicate your strong desire to break free from feeling trapped. In Alcoholics Anonymous groups, one often hears the phrase: "If you don't know the day you took your last drink, you probably haven't." There's a value to remembering *when* something changed in our lives. May I suggest that as a phrase of truth (often highlighted or given as a course of action) hits your heart with the sound of a turning key and the creaking hinges of an opening door, write in the margin the date you read it and the words, "Thank you, Lord."

1 -Trapped by Confused Thinking
. . . Up Until Now

What a strange pattern the shuttle
of life can weave.

Francis Marion

When you and I feel trapped — either
physically or mentally — the first reaction of the body or mind is to panic,
to want to get out, to remove ourselves from what has suddenly become a threatening situation. Your
trap could be a car accident, a fearful
walk down a dark alley, an unwanted
stay in the hospital, or a destructive
relationship. It could be a situation

set up by choices to overeat and not exercise, or to avoid mental challenges. It could be a dead-end job, or a difficult family, or an income that is never enough. You feel trapped. Immobilized. Panicked.

To turn on the lights in our minds — the first step in getting out of our entrapment — means to turn on a new way of thinking about ourselves, others and the world in which we live. If we keep thinking what we've always thought, we will keep getting what we've always got. Our new choice is to change our attitude, our thinking, which means to begin to see things in different and more exciting ways.

David Thought Differently

I know you remember the story of a most unlikely teenager and his choice to fight the great Philistine giant Goliath. Big job. Scary job. But David's even larger challenge was to combat the negative, faithless thinking of his own people, battalions of whom should have been his cheering section. Instead, ringing in David's ears were words that must have sounded something like, "Hey, boy, you haven't got a chance. Can't you see how big that guy is? He's huge. He's going to slam dunk you into the earth. He's too big, and you're too small!" How would you feel if you were "trapped" in such a situation? You're out there putting your life on the line, and all you hear is fear and frustration from those who were supposed to be your staunch supporters. I can't imagine you would be very happy.

But David was an amazing boy. What did he do? He chose a different way to look at his precarious situation. He was not intimidated nor did he feel all alone. As he fingered a single, smooth stone in his sling, calculated the distance between himself and Goliath's broad forehead, which glistened in the Israel sun, David must have thought, *Yes, he's big. Real big. In fact, he's so big there's no way that I can miss.* Same giant. Same threat to Israel. Just a different point of view. And we all know the result of David's different thinking. Down came Goliath, and at once victory was delivered into the timid hearts of the children of Israel.

Beware the Status Quo
Conventional thinking suggested

that the thousands of warriors standing at the ready would be the key to Israel's victory over the Philistines. After all, haven't we always been told there's strength in numbers? In this case, it was faith in a big God and the *attitude* of a young boy that won the day. So much for statistics. Large numbers — or the narrow view of the strong and powerful — are seldom the key to victory. It's how we think that makes the difference.

Here are some examples of people's past thinking — not all that long ago — which seemed sensible at the time:

While theoretically and technically television may be feasible, commercially and financially I consider it an impossibility, a development of which we need

waste little time dreaming.
> Lee De Forest, U.S. inventor,
> "Father of the Radio," 1926

As far as sinking a ship with a bomb is concerned, you just can't do it.
> Rear Admiral Clark Woodard,
> U. S. Navy, 1939

Face it, Louis. Civil War pictures have never made a dime.
> Irving Thalberg,
> MGM producer,
> advising his boss Louis B. Mayer
> against buying the rights to
> *Gone with the Wind*

In their times, the counsels of De Forest, Woodard and Thalberg seemed to make sense. But history proved them wrong. Dead wrong. Let's fast forward history to your life and mine today. Do we have some of this murky thinking in our own minds? If so, then the first step in getting out of our own entrapments and tunnel vision must also be to change our thinking and our attitudes about our situations. So here we go. We're trapped and we don't like it. We're tired of the physical and emotional drain our problems are taking on our lives. We're also frustrated, annoyed and desperate enough to take a look at some new directions.

TAKE ACTION

To begin to make the first move from "I'm trapped" to "I'm free to make other choices," we must understand and believe the truth of one sentence. The Bible puts it this way: "For as he thinks in his heart, so is he" (Proverbs 23:7, NKJV). Our actions follow our thinking — conscious or unconscious. If we don't like what our lives are producing, it would be a good idea to check and see what kinds of crops we are planting. This is why the Bible talks so much about the law of sowing and reaping. If you think crazy thoughts, you reap crazy results. If you live with the idea that says, *Woe is me, I'm trapped forever,* then guess what? *You're trapped forever.*

In realizing that *thinking* and *attitude* are key words for the choice of changed behavior, a friend of mine has framed on his desk the following words of Chuck Swindoll:

The biggest part of any problem is the way I choose to think about it.

The longer I live, the more I realize the impact of attitude on life. Attitude, to me, is more important than facts. It is more important than the past, than education, than money, than circumstances, than failures, than successes, than what other people think or do. It is more important than appearances, giftedness or skill. It will make or break a company, a church, a home. The remarkable thing is that I have a choice every day regarding the attitude I will embrace for that day. I cannot change my past. . . . I cannot change the fact that people will act in a certain way. I cannot change the inevitable. The only think I can do is play on the one string I have, and that is my attitude. I am convinced that life is ten percent what happens to me and ninety percent how I react to it.

If we think our problems are absolutely horrible and unsolvable, then that's the way they will be. When we think they are solvable and growable, then that's the way they will be. It all depends on how we think.

Stinking Thinking

Let me tell you about Norma. She was sixty pounds overweight and desperately unhappy. As she sat in my office lamenting her ever-widening girth, she said, "Dr. Freed, my problem is that I just can't lose weight. It's pure and simple, I just can't do it. And when I do lose a little, I put it right back on. It always happens that way. I'll just always be fat." That is how Norma always defined her problem. But that was *not* her problem at all. It only *became* her problem because she kept telling herself it was her problem. It's something motivational speakers would refer to as *stinking thinking.*

Norma repeatedly told herself, *I can't do it. I'm incapable of change. I make a little progress, but then I fall back. It's hopeless. I always do this.* She had become so accustomed to saying this that it was second nature. But when she learned to say, "Up until now this is what I've done, but now I've found a new way to do what I want," she started to do exactly that. Here is a life principle to help put the issue at center stage: Only as you tell yourself something is going to continue to be a problem can the problem keep on being your problem.

Some of the most interesting studies of the human mind in the last few years involve our understanding of the function of the left and right parts of the brain. Here we make decisions regarding what we see as *truth*. A thought comes into your mind and enters your *left* brain as *fact* — much like a book that's just been catalogued in your mental library. Your library, which loves to receive new material, accepts the new arrival as unquestioned, undeniable truth. This is your basic data, much like $E=mc^2$, or $2+2 = 4$. But it doesn't stop there. There is a point at which a greater truth springs to life.

Sometimes we call this an *aha!* experience. This is when the information, once the exclusive property of the left brain, moves over into the right brain. Now those *facts* become laced with emotion, understanding and human experience. They are shaped and massaged into *facts with meaning*. This is what the Bible refers to as *believing with the heart*. It means that truth has come alive, and we begin to see things as they really are. Immediately, the words come to our lips, "I see," and we enjoy a never-to-be-forgotten *aha!* experience.

If I recite a portion of John 3:16 to you — "For God so loved the world that he gave his only Son" — that is history and information. Fact. Left-brain information. But the information has moved to the right brain when you are able to say, *It's almost unbelievable that God loves me and that he has come into my world, that he knows me by name, that I'm special to him, and that he loves me unconditionally.* What was once a verbal statement becomes a vital reality in your life. Your right-brain heart has infused it with emotion and life experience. From that day forward nothing is ever the same again.

Suddenly talk moves to walk. Facts, once sterile words on a time-worn page, now move on in faith to the pages of your life. Your left brain reads the map, but your right brain takes the trip, and what a wonderful, wild roller-coaster adventure it is. But now this poses a problem for us because we also know the heart can be deceitful. Our choices in life can be filled with truth and understanding or with lies and misunderstanding. When we choose deception and deceit, we call this a denial of the truth. Our heart — that right-brain part of us — is an expert at playing games with us.

Finding Out What You Already Know

One of my patients, whom I will call Sally, sat in my office after just learning her husband was having an affair. Pushing back her tears she said to me, "Why is it the wife is always the last to know?"

My response was, "It actually surprises me that you ask that question, because in our previous sessions you shared some significant things with me. Just last week you told me your husband had been at a church board meeting until four o'clock in the morning. Now I'm sure that could have raised a few questions in your mind, enough to at least to have said to one of the wives of the other board members, 'Whew, that must have been some meeting last night!' You would probably have heard her say, 'I don't know. My husband was home by nine-thirty,' and you would then have known something was going on with your husband. You simply passed that information on to me, thinking it was important for me to know about it, but you said nothing more about it. Now I'm surprised you think you were the last to know your husband was having an affair."

There were a couple of minutes of silence while Sally struggled deep within herself. Finally, she said, "Dr.

Freed, this may sound crazy, but I really *did* know. I've known for a long time that my husband was having an affair."

Silence did its own work. Finally, out of that quietness she offered, "I know who the woman is, too. She's my best friend." Still, Sally spoke of this with a strange, almost unreal sense of wonder. She asked me, "How could I have known and still not known?" It's the kind of question you and I have asked ourselves a hundred times or more about any number of situations. And it is this issue with which we are grappling in this chapter. How, why, and when do we choose the *thinking* we choose? Sally's husband was confident that the grass was greener on the other side. What he didn't know is that the grass is *never* greener on the other side.

TAKE ACTION

The only place the grass is greener is *where we choose to water it*. The grass is greener wherever we choose to take control of our thoughts. The grass is greener when we are honest with our thoughts. The grass is greener when we keep our promises and honor our commitments. Then we understand when the Bible says the *heart* — our right brain — must be guarded diligently. That's why you and I must take good care of our hearts, for out of our hearts flow the issues of life.

There's a story about a traveler who came to a crossroads on the outskirts of a small town. He inquired of one of the townspeople what kind of citizens lived in the village.

"What kind of people live in the town where you've come from?" asked the townsman.

"Suspicious people, and not terribly trustworthy," said the traveler.

"Ah, and that is indeed whom you will find here," said the townsman.

A few minutes later, yet another traveler came to the crossroads. She, too, inquired of the local citizen what manner of people lived in the village.

"What kind of people would you expect to find?" asked the townsman.

"Kind and generous men and women who have open hearts and who welcome strangers, I would think," replied the woman.

"Ah, and that is indeed whom you

will find over yonder hill," said the citizen.

Now we are "seeing" more clearly the truth we addressed earlier: The biggest part of any problem is the way you and I choose to think about it. Let me illustrate further with this intriguing story.

Two Views, One Family

Two boys grew up in an alcoholic home where both parents were constantly under the influence. Now grown men, one went on to become a business success. He was also a nondrinker. His brother's life became just the opposite, with continuing personal and financial disaster, and an addiction to alcohol. The two brothers were interviewed separately, at which time each was asked this question: To what do you attribute your style of living? Their response was fascinating. Each man answered with the same words. "Well, with my background, what would you expect?" Same family history, different individual decisions. One chose the role of victim: *How could I not drink?* The other chose the role of conqueror: *Why in the world, with that background, would I want to drink?*

TAKE ACTION
What does this story have to do with how you and I choose our thinking? Our choice of thoughts determines whether we are exercising our *own* control and power or allowing others — even those long dead — to call the shots in our lives. So

what happens when we decide to *take back* our power and begin to live from the inside out? A whole new world of love and freedom opens to us, and that's when we really begin to live!

When I was a boy growing up on a block in Washington, D.C., a couple lived a few doors down from me. This couple could neither speak nor hear. While this disability created certain challenges in their lives, it did not keep them from being gainfully employed at the United States Printing Office. Their lives were actually quite normal, except for one unique part of their home. Instead of a doorbell, they had a button for a door light. It was great fun to run up on the porch at night — with girls watching, of course — and push that button. All the lights in the house would go on, and the husband would burst out carrying a baseball bat. As he swung wildly at our heads, furious, upset, and ready to knock our blocks off, we would duck, dodge and run. It was great fun, and extremely mean. We *acted,* and the man *reacted,* and as long as that pattern of behavior continued, we could entertain ourselves well into the Washington night.

Any behavior that repeats itself
is being rewarded.

One evening, I remember a little girl was standing there, and I wanted to impress her. Knowing the couple was at home, I pushed the door-light button. But this time no one came to the door. No swinging baseball bat.

No angry man fuming and carrying on. I pushed the button again, poised to run off into the night. But no one came. I pushed a couple more times, then, in frustration, I pushed it one last time. No response, and no more fun. In a moment, this man took back his power and control. He chose to think and act differently about his problem. He won. I lost.

He thought, *If I don't react to those kids, I bet they'll quit pushing the button.* He was right. He may not have been able to articulate it, but he was actually living out our key truth that says: Any behavior that repeats itself is being rewarded. As naughty little boys we were being rewarded by his coming to the door when we pushed the button. When he quit, we quit. He had taken away our reward.

Whom Can You Change?

A woman recently came to me for counseling. Before even sitting down, she was well into her list of grievances with, "Do you know what makes me angry? My ex-husband is always late when he picks up the kids."

I asked her, "Well, what do you do when he comes late?"

She replied, "I always get really angry and blow up at him. And yet, the next time, there he is late again. It just keeps happening."

I suggested that at the heart of this conflict were the issues of power and control, which probably contributed significantly to their divorce. He was choosing to be late, and she was choosing to let him upset her. This gave him the same power and control he had exerted in their marriage. This was his reward — the sense of control he got from knowing he had upset her. But now she was about to learn she had another choice, one based on this simple thought: *The only person I can change is myself.*

So with a little instruction, she chose to move from being a reactor (under his control) to a relator (under her control). She chose to remove the reward he got from making her angry. On his next tardy arrival, she re-marked, "Wow, I'm glad you were late tonight. It really helped me get some things done with the kids. I had more time than I've ever had before. Thanks." The next time he was on time. What happened? She changed the only person she *could* change. That meant he had to change, too, because he was dealing with a different person. The only way to "change" another person's actions is to change ourselves. If we choose not to do this and keep pushing the other person instead, that person will push back in resistance. It's the law of cause and effect.

TAKE ACTION

Right now, you have the freedom to choose to believe that the only person you can change is the one reading these words. All of this has to do with your attitude, which is your way of seeing things. You are changing your life every time you think, *Ah, I see it!* This chapter — and this book — is all about altering your view of yourself and others.

We began this book with wisdom

taken from Proverbs 23: For as a person thinks in the heart, so he or she is. It was no different for those who read the Proverbs when they were first written than it is for us today: If we think, *I can't,* we will be right. If we think, *I can,* we also will be right. Whichever way we choose to think, that we will become. Here's a classic example of this thinking.

The only person I can change
is <u>myself.</u>

A member of a local church came to me for professional counsel. His problem? His wife. In this and a subsequent session I heard all about her problems. Shortly before his third appointment, my secretary buzzed me to pickup my phone. I did, and a woman's voice came through. "Dr. Freed, I hear a member of my church has been seeing you. I sing in the church choir. He and I have been meeting together in a motel twice a week for the last year. I'm afraid he's not telling you about this."

During the session that day the man continued to berate his wife. At one point, I leaned toward him, squinting my eyes. He was upset and asked me what I was doing. I squinted some more. By now, he was enraged.

"Stop doing that, it upsets me," he said. "What are you doing, anyway?"

I said, "I'm thinking."

"Well, what are you thinking?" he asked.

"I'm thinking that you are not telling me the truth."

He stood up abruptly, went to the

door, and was about to storm out of my office.

"You're supposed to be a loving Christian counselor and you talk to me like that? I'm leaving," he said.

"And you're a member in a local church and you've been seeing a woman from your church choir at a local hotel twice each week?" I asked.

Silence. The man had been confronted with the truth. He sat down, and for the first time we were able to have an honest conversation. The man now had the opportunity to choose the way he would think. Up until then no healing was possible. He had to touch the truth, and the truth had to touch him.

Thinking, Rewards and Change

King David, in biblical times, had

an affair with a married neighbor named Bathsheba. She became pregnant. Her husband, a soldier, was fighting in a war. David, the supreme commander, ordered him to be put into the most fierce fighting. He was killed, and David married his widow. Now David had committed the sins of both adultery and murder. He covered this over and told no one. Months later, a prophet of God named Nathan asked David what he thought should be done to a rich man who steals the only sheep of a poor man and kills it.

David replied, "The man should be stoned to death."

Nathan responded, "And you are the man!" Confronted with his sin, David chose to change his heart through tearful sorrow and repentance. Later, God even called David "a man after my own heart." This is what we call *amazing grace*.

You now have been introduced to three powerful truths on which you can build your thinking:

- The most important part of my problem is how I think about it.
- Whatever anyone does repeatedly is being rewarded.
- The only person I can change is myself.

With these truths you are beginning to recognize the wrong choices that have trapped you in your life *up until now*. Perhaps you've not yet gotten over some of those choices. There is still time, there is still hope, and there is still a loving God. How will this happen? Well, I trust it already has started. But we have much more to say, and some of the answers are waiting for you in the next chapter. Read on with an open mind and an ever-opening heart.

What If You Can't?

After reading an early version of this book manuscript, a good friend of mine replied:

There is something that bothers me about the main thesis of this book, and it would be a shame to ignore it. It seems to me that there are still people who simply can't do the things you describe. For whatever reason — brain abnormalities, biochemical imbalances — the deck is stacked against them. Some people are more prepared than others, genetically and biologically (as well as circumstantially), to take life by the tail. Those less fortunate might manifest a depression through fits of temper, a gloomy disposition, always seeing the glass as half full, or thinking, *I can't*. Treat the medical problem and often that person's outlook will change and suddenly that person declares, *"I can!"*

I can think of a client who perfectly illustrates this point. George (not his real name) was about twenty-five when he came to see me for psychotherapy. My case notes of the initial sessions contained a lot of quotations:

- "I've been a loser all my life."
- "I can't get a job or go to school because I'll make mistakes and everybody will laugh at me."
- "I hate being with people because they always ask me what I'm doing. Do I just say, 'Nothing'?"
- "I don't like having to live with my parents, and they don't like it either."

My notes also listed a number of behaviors and feelings that George reported:

- Favorite activities no longer bring him joy
- Has withdrawn from friends
- Feels hopeless, worthless, guilty (due to his Christian convictions,

he says, "I shouldn't feel this way")
- Poor concentration
- Indecisiveness
- Impulsive, little understanding of the value of putting off one thing in order to have something better later on (delayed gratification)
- Some suicidal thoughts but no plan of action

After these initial sessions, I offered George my assessment. I told him that I thought he was suffering from a clinical depression, depressed feelings caused in part by a chemical deficiency in the brain. I also suspected that he had an adult form of ADHD, Attention Deficit/Hyperactivity Disorder.

George's parents, whom he had invited to this session, contributed the information that George had been called hyperactive by all of his teachers, starting in kindergarten. His father said, "My teachers said the same thing about me. I used to have all kinds of trouble the way he does." This made me wonder about a possible genetic link.

I referred George to a psychiatrist for further assessment and treatment with antidepressant medication. George also got involved in a group for adults with ADHD. And he and I continued to meet for several more sessions.

Today George is taking college classes at night and attending a Sunday school class that integrates the truths of the Bible with the truths of psychology. He is learning about himself, and he no longer sees himself as a loser. With the medication, George was able to put to use many of the insights he was learning in psychotherapy, Sunday school and his ADHD group. I doubt he could have done all of this without medication.

George confronted a physiological problem related to brain chemicals, and he accepted the curing power of a psychotropic medicine. God had led physicians to discover the healing powers of this medication, just as God has been present in all discoveries of medical methods of healing.

In suggesting that our thinking has an enormous impact on our outlook on life, I am not ignoring that there are obvious physiological factors in some emotional disturbances.

George's form of depression could be called "endogenous" because it came from within his body. Six weeks after combating his malfunctioning, trapped and negative attitudes with God-given medication, I saw George singing merrily at a men's gathering at our church.

Let me put all of this in another perspective. I believe that most of the time we are fully responsible for what we feel by choosing the thoughts we choose. Thus, at least fifty-one percent of the time we are making a choice. But the other forty-nine percent of the time, some other factors may come into play, such as:

- Emotional instability due to a troublesome thyroid gland
- Mood swings that accompany

the illness labeled "manic-depressive" or "bipolar," which can be due to an insufficient level of lithium in the body
- Depression caused by hormonal factors, such as childbirth
- Possible hereditarily low levels of chemicals in the brain that would normally help one to feel hopeful
- The side effects of certain types of medications
- The metabolic differences that seem to be associated with ADHD

One woman, marveling at the improvement of her husband after his bipolar disorder was treated with lithium, said, "I so thank God for giving you wisdom that my husband could be healed by God-created lithium." When emotional problems have a medical base, then a change in thinking is not the only thing that is needed. Medical problems usually need medical treatment. Don't hesitate to seek such treatment if the suggestions made in this book seem completely impossible for you to carry out.

2 -Trapped by My Persistent Past
. . . Up Until Now

> Wisdom never kicks at the iron walls it can't bring down.
>
> Olive Schreiner

There was a soldier who bore my name and my serial number in World War II. From the terror of pitched battle on the European front, he emerged barely alive with a leg twisted backward and a bleeding stump of an arm. When he awakened in a battlefield hospital, his first thought was that he had had a bad dream — a terrible nightmare. Convinced he hadn't been hurt after all, he moved the fingers on his right hand. Then he felt an itch between those fingers and reached out to scratch it. The fingers weren't there. This introduction to his "phantom arm" was both overwhelming and devastating. He had to mourn the loss of his limb and adjust to becoming a southpaw.

It was a few days after this shattering realization that a wise person grabbed hold of my heart. I will never forget the impact. A fellow soldier looked me in the eye and smiled and said, "Frank, the experience you have just gone through will either make you a bitter person or a better person. The choice is completely up to you." As I lay on the cot in that military hospital, I linked those words with God's counsel that "all things work together for good." That's when I called on divine guidance to help me make the right decision. Would I become bitter or better? More aware or angrier? Positive or pessimistic? I'm grateful that God gave me the courage to make the right choice. Many of the wounded lying around me did not make that positive choice, and I'm in no position to give their reasons why. But I still can see their faces in my mind's eye many decades later . . . so many of my wounded buddies who chose to be trapped in the *bitter*.

Bitter or Better?

It is no secret that the quality of our lives is determined by the sum of our choices. When we feel trapped, in more cases than not, it is because we have made choices that have played out into situations that are causing us grief or discomfort. However, most people do not see this. They often continue in their unhappiness with their predicament, but they seldom attempt to understand how they trapped themselves in the first place. We now know that the most effective way to get untrapped is to revisit those initial choices, briefly relive them, and then release (dismiss) them from memory. *Briefly* and *release* are the key words here. The only reason to dig into the past is for insight into our present, after that we must move on. If we are unwilling to go through this often difficult process, then the old adage will remain true: *That which we resist, will persist.*

A gentle re-reading of our personal history is important. It's our blueprint, our emotional DNA, and every bit as important as a doctor's records are for understanding the state of our physical health. The past always yields clues to the present, and only when we know how we got to where we are can we begin to understand who we are and where we are headed.

Whatever your pain, fear, hurt or sadness, you can make the choice
to be bitter or better.

Your life circumstances may not have been chosen by you, but the direction of your life can be. You may have thought it impossible to make

70

that choice, or perhaps you hoped that someone else might conveniently show up and make the decision for you. That's what you may have thought . . . *up until now*. You now know that the decision is yours to use your past, troubled though it may have been, as either a teacher or an excuse. I wonder what it will be for you. So many people I see day after day continue to allow the unpleasant experiences of their past to influence their present thoughts, which is a perfect formula for staying trapped and an efficient model for remaining unhappy and unfulfilled.

It's difficult to keep out negative, nonproductive thoughts, but there is a great difference between *having* a thought and *nurturing* a thought. One is natural; the other is intentional.

Therein lies an important difference.

In cases of posttraumatic stress disorder, flashbacks of horrible scenes may continue to play on the large screens of our minds. It's happened to me off and on for more than fifty years as my experiences on the battlefield throw their full-color pictures on the walls of my mind. Panic attacks may seem to signify a horrible death when triggered by some "close call" experience in the present. As we have already seen, it is only a short step to allowing the past to regulate our present. The good news I want to share with you in these pages is: You no longer need to live out of control, trapped by a distant, and no longer existing, past.

Be Gentle on Yourself

What happens when we modify our attitudes about the past by being less tough on ourselves and, actually, more realistic with the truth? The first, and more honest, thing we must be prepared to admit is that *we cannot change our past.* What has been done is done. Emotional health and healing come about when we let go of the *if onlys* and *yes, buts* of regret, remorse and recrimination. We don't have to love our past or even like it, but it is good mental health to accept it. It is only at this moment of acceptance that we will be freed to behave differently in the here and now, no longer choosing to be controlled by the then and when.

For a moment I want you to enter the inner confines of the remote control on your television set — a ready-made example of what we're talking about. Take the remote control you use nightly to banish loud commercials and begin moving quickly channel to channel, program to program, news to music, sitcom to documentary.

Remote-Controlling Your Past

Now start to reframe the TV remote control as a remote control for your thinking. Picture something agitating, disconcerting, sad, shrill, or unfriendly and *zap* it. Presto. It's gone. You've suddenly changed channels, replacing that image or sequence of events or old internal tape with a different image. What do you see? Have you not created a new set of circumstances for yourself? And did you not do it quickly? In a flash? And if you still don't like what's on the screen of your mind, keep channel surfing.

TAKE ACTION

Since there is no such thing as an actual mental remote control, I have many of my patients wear rubber bands on their wrists to help them "change channels." As they consciously monitor their thinking, sooner or later an unwanted, unrequested thought from the past invades their minds, and they *snap* the rubber band. Not with enough force to inflict pain, but with enough sting to get their attention. What does this experience tell them? That with this rubbery reminder they can *change* their thinking simply by being *aware* of their thinking. It triggers the thought, *Let it go*. And guess what? It goes. Every time. After all, who wants to feel the endless, irritating snap of a rubber band!

A young man — I'll call him John — was involved in a chain-reaction accident involving cars colliding at a high rate of speed on a crowded Los Angeles freeway. His car was hit on all four sides, and he could not get out of it. The automobile next to him was immediately engulfed in flames. While helplessly waiting and praying for aid, John watched and heard a man on fire in the next car, burning to death. In my office a short time later, John said to me, "I'll never get that picture out of my mind. It was so terrible. I still feel guilty about it, even though I couldn't get out to help him."

After several sessions of rehearsed self-talk, John began to learn a new way to think about what he'd seen, and he soon was wearing a rubber band to help him get through each day despite being overstimulated by that terrible event. After snapping himself more than forty times the first day, he progressively dealt with his reaction to the accident, until on the twenty-ninth day he was finally free. When I asked him if the event was still disturbing him, he replied, "Not at all. Every so often I just use my 'mental remote' and I move on."

There Is a Way Out!
From this story we discover there is at least one more important thing to

help us find release from whatever our trapped condition might be. Before coming to see me, John told me on the phone that he'd tried his best to tell himself he shouldn't *think* about the accident. But whenever he did this, matters just got worse. He would panic, become depressed, feel more guilt and otherwise have a very bad day. What my young friend didn't know was that it's simply not possible to bury a feeling. It just won't die. It may, in fact, become more alive than ever. There it is, buried deep in the ground, seemingly harmless, all the while it is turning over and over in its shallow grave until the feeling finally breaks through, saying, "I'm back!" In fact, it had never left. I explained to John that the more you fight a feeling, the stronger it becomes. Feelings love resistance. The more you push, the more they push back, giving credence to the truth that the *shoulds* and *shouldn'ts* of life not only prove themselves useless, but are guaranteed to be counterproductive.

TAKE ACTION

We've talked about releasing the past from our minds and consequently from our thoughts. The key to getting out of your trap and moving through the pain of the past is to engage in the active verb *supersede*. The dictionary defines this word as "to remove something by putting something else in its place." How do you do this? The required action on your part is to empower the new — what you know is truth today — and to force out the old with its pain and despair. Put another way, to see a dramatic change for good in your future means you must go well beyond where you've ever traveled before. Much like Christopher Columbus, who superseded the Old World for the New World, you, too, will be required to risk embracing today's new reality and allowing it to supersede your past. You can't live in a static past *and* enjoy the dynamic present. They cannot coexist. Columbus would not have discovered the New World had he never taken the risk (of falling off the edge of the flat world) and headed for new lands on the high seas. The good news is that you, too, can become your own pioneer as you make even more important discoveries in *your* new world. (More on Columbus later.)

The Forgiveness Factor

How do we put this search for your own "New World" into action? After decades of being a counselor, I've come to the conclusion that the most effective way to heal the wounds, anger, fears and hurts of the past is to learn how to forgive. The prominent theologian and writer Dr. Lewis Smedes tells of a lady who one day received a phone call from her exhusband who had left her a few years earlier to marry his secretary. The former husband told her he had found new faith in God and said, "I would like to ask you to forgive me."

With a heart full of bitterness this woman told Dr. Smedes, "And I said

81

to him, 'I would like to ask you to go straight to the devil.'"

Not an uncommon response, you might say. Maybe even the *right* response, given the circumstances. But let's look deeper. Who is being hurt here? And by whom? Obviously the ex-wife was nursing her bitterness to her own destruction. But did the man deserve forgiveness? After all, he's the one who flew the coop. Did the woman deserve what he did to her, with all those long nights of seething hatred and painful days when she wished her faithless spouse would just disappear from the face of the earth? Did either of them *deserve* release from the bad, painful memories of a relationship that was no more? No, but they certainly needed such a release. Could anyone — should anyone — try to persuade the wronged wife to change her attitude? Yes. But not for his sake — *for hers*. I'm sure she would like to stop the hurting if only someone would show her how. To forgive him for her sake would be superseding old, bitter thoughts by substituting the better thoughts of getting on with her life.

Failure Is Not a Person

This leads us to the awareness that if our lives are to be rich and full, we also must learn to forgive ourselves. Too often you and I dwell needlessly on our past failures — what we could have done better, how we might have been more patient, more loving, more understanding, and how we should have held our tongue. Thoughts lacking moral courage may have prompted actions that lacked integrity, and we have allowed those past events to haunt our memories and brand us failures. *Up until now.* Now we can bring a fresh, new understanding to that which has trapped us for so long. We are learning that "failure" in the past was an event, not a person. It was something we did, not something we were. Do you remember how, as kids, we would spend hours outdoors focusing the heat of the sun through a magnifying glass on a dried leaf until it burned to ashes? In the same way, right now, you and I can take each leaf of a painful, haunting memory, hold it to the magnifying glass of our new way of thinking, and say, *Lord, forgive me and make me clean. Burn up my desire to focus on the events* of the past that are keeping me from being the person you designed me to be. It is not your will that I remain trapped in my past. Burn through the debris of my past and in your divine providence blow away the ashes.

3 - Trapped by Self-Sabotaging Fear
. . . Up Until Now

I can do everything through [Christ] who gives me strength.

Philippians 4:13

One of the strangest aspects of the human heart is its ability both to build its greatest dreams and to destroy them. Most of us have grieved over the death of a dream. One's heart, timing itself negatively, is a master at "snatching defeat out of the jaws of success," as one fractured cliché puts it. To our lips comes the astounding question: "How could I have done that? I knew better! I just seem to have sabotaged everything I really wanted." And to this kind of thinking, I as a therapist respond: "You can trace all this to fear in your heart that cancels out love."

One way of defining human emotions relationally is this:

- Love moves toward a person, place or thing
- Fear moves away from a person, place or thing
- Anger moves against a person, place or thing

With this definition in mind, perhaps we can better understand the civil war between love and fear that rages in the human heart. When we keep taking a step forward (love) and then a step backward (fear), we become immobilized, going nowhere. This leads to feelings of frustration, which is most often the basis of anger. And anger most often causes us to move against ourselves.

Fear the Enemy of the Light

The Bible comes straight to the point in 1 John 4:18 when it reminds us that "there is no fear in love. But perfect love drives out fear, because fear has to do with punishment. The one who fears is not made perfect in love." Just as deep, ominous darkness is an enemy of light, so fear darkens love, resulting in a midnight of the soul that approaches what we know as depression.

It's interesting that the first time

the word *hide* appears in the Bible is when God speaks to Adam, saying, "Where are you?"

Adam's response is, "I was afraid, and hid myself." What unwitting psychological honesty by the world's first person! And as that pathology has been passed on to future strugglers, we have continued to see fear, especially in insecure relationships where two people hide themselves from each other. In this anxious environment with its masks, pretense and disguises, individuals are not *relating* at all. They might call it a relationship, but they are only *reacting* to each other. In such a "reactionship" no one is saying, "I love you for all the good things in me that you bring out." Hiding never brings out the best in us. It only teaches us the tragic art of denial, which means to not see things the way they really are.

There can be no healthy, productive relationships when the only foundation is fear. In the biblical story of creation, Adam and Eve were not only hiding from God, but they also were hiding from each other and blaming each other. Our world's first couple never learned the truth that as long as you fix the blame on somebody, you can't fix the problem in yourself. Fear and blame go hand in hand. Whereas the Bible says that perfect love drives out fear, those of us in Adam and Eve's skin live with the belief that perfect denial will save us from blame. Why do we keep trying to fool ourselves? It's not denial that wins the day; it's love's loyalty to one's self that faces the truth and learns how to handle it productively.

As long as you fix the blame on somebody, you can't fix the problem in yourself.

Now we can understand why biblical wisdom urges that we, "Above all else, guard [our] affections. For they influence everything else in our lives" (Proverbs 4:23, TLB). When we guard our hearts, we protect our valuables: our valuable mind, emotions and beliefs, our valuable relationships with God and one another. So we must be careful what we set our hearts on: on fear, we get it; on love, we get it, too. The fact is that if we make the unwise choice of setting our hearts on both fear and love, we end up trapped. This is why, when Solomon was asked by God what he most needed, Solomon responded, "an understanding heart."

Trapped by a Fearful Past

When we invite fear into our hearts, we create minds filled with frustration, anxiety and pain. From this we become angry and move against somebody. Initially, that "somebody" is ourselves.

Now, we must ask ourselves, just how does fear get into our emotional bloodstream? This happens when, as noted previously, the language of fear comes into our thoughts, saying, "Yes, I would like to, but . . ." In such a simple phrase, there is at first an expressed intention that sounds like someone moving toward something

when it says, "Yes, I would like to."
Then, like lowering a voice or like
pressing the delete key on a computer
keyboard, there follows the word *but.*
One step forward, one step back.
This is what we mean by being
trapped in the *status quo,* a Latin
phrase that means "the way things
are." Everything grinds to a halt with
just six words, "Yes, I would like to,
but . . ."

TAKE ACTION

Think back for a moment about the
college you might have attended or
the person you might have married or
the career you might have pursued
or the investment you might have
made. You didn't because of that terrible little phrase. Think how those

six words have helped build the person in which you voluntarily locked yourself. Could it possibly be that the key for getting out might be found in eliminating those words from your vocabulary and from your mind? This can be done by reframing your thoughts to say: *Up until now, I have felt trapped.* Sooner or later, you can reach this point.

Still, you may be thinking, *But my parents argued and broke up and I no longer had a daddy to love me, to play with me, and to make me feel good about myself. I'm afraid that if I love someone today, as I loved my father, I will again be abandoned. Yes, I'd really like to change, but . . . !*

TAKE ACTION

I understand your fear, and I want to help with some positive suggestions. Pause, think for a while, and then write for a few minutes about some of these painful experiences in you life. Perhaps early on you were promised things that important people in your life never delivered. You'd get your expectations up about a promise that was made to you, only to see your dreams crumble. Unfortunately, it happened again and again, until you actually developed a habit of expecting the worst. Because of those unhappy experiences, perhaps you taught yourself not to count on good things happening in your life. To this day you may still be thinking negative and fearful thoughts about success, your health, or your general well-being. You might even destroy something good so another person can't let you down. You keep setting yourself up for failure when a loving God designed you to succeed.

Another way to understand being trapped by our fears and uncontrolled emotions is to think about one specific period in our world's history. Pretend you are a citizen in the fifteenth century. You and all those who live in your world are what we would call "flat earth" people. Cartographers have brilliantly mapped the contours of Europe. Shorelines have been studied and "accurately" inscribed on maps. You have been told the world is flat. In fact, as you looked closely, you could see something written on the edges of these maps. They are the words: "Beyond this there be dragons." How interesting. Dragons. Danger. Fear of the unknown. A call to be careful, cautious. The maps gave you fair warning not to sail too far out into uncharted waters or you'd find yourself in trouble from which there will be no escape. Then something happens.

"In 1492, Columbus sailed the ocean blue." His trip to the New World was simply *faith making new maps*. Dragons? Columbus didn't think so. The dragons were figments of someone's creative imagination.

I Was Filled with Fear . . . Up Until Now!

Can't you just hear the conversation Columbus had with the flat world people? They might say, "Christopher, what do you think you're doing anyway? What happens when you fall off the edge?"

To this the great discoverer surely must have responded, "I used to worry about that . . . up until now." Columbus had already written the first pages of this book. He knew what you are now learning, that fear means overestimating your risks and under-estimating your resources.

When imperial Rome was the mighty superpower on planet earth, her leaders boasted that if there was no way, they would make a way! Robert Schuller picks up this thought in a Christian context by telling people to say, "When faced with a mountain, I will not quit. I will keep on striving until I climb over, find a passage through, or simply stay and turn the mountain into a gold mine, with God's help."

The good news is that you are no longer alone in your decision-making process — even though at times you feel no good decision can be made. I promise you that your loving heavenly Father can and will provide you a clear direction. Here is a beautiful little story that illustrates my point, told by Edward de Bono in his book *New Think*.

Many years ago when a person who owed money could be thrown into jail, a merchant in London had the misfortune to owe a huge sum to a money-lender. The money-lender, who was old and ugly, fancied the merchant's beautiful teenage daughter. He proposed a bargain. He said he would cancel the merchant's debt if he could have the girl instead.

Both the merchant and his daughter were horrified at the proposal. So the cunning money-lender proposed that they let Providence decide the matter. He told them that he would put a black pebble into an empty money-bag and then the girl would have to pick out one of the pebbles. If she chose the black pebble she would become his wife and her father's debt would be canceled. If she chose the white pebble she would stay with her father and the debt would still be canceled. But if she refused to pick out a pebble, her father would be thrown into jail and she would starve.

Reluctantly the merchant agreed. They were standing on a pebble-strewn path in the merchant's garden as they talked, and the money-lender stooped down to pick up the two pebbles. As he picked up the pebbles, the girl, sharp-eyed with fright, noticed that he picked up two black pebbles and put them into the money-bag. He then asked the girl to pick out the pebble that was to decide her fate and that of her father. . . .

[Then the girl] put her hand into the money-bag and drew out a pebble. Without looking at it she fumbled and let it fall to the path where it was immediately lost among all the others.

101

"Oh, how clumsy of me," she said, "but never mind — if you look into the bag you will be able to tell which pebble I took by the color of the one that is left."

Partners in Pain

What happened in this little story that you can relate to your life? Just like the girl, you have known the hopeless feeling of being stuck in a situation where there seemed to be neither a way out nor a way in. There have been times when you felt trapped in situations, when you felt you simply could not win. I know your fears, because I've been there, too. That makes us partners in pain. Permit me to be very personal here. When I first started my studies in psychology, I felt a deep need to relate my new understanding to my former studies in theology. At that time, I was also in a trapped place in my life. I could see no exit signs. There were no escape hatches. But I became intrigued with the second book of the Bible — the book of Exodus, which in Hebrew means "a way out." Out of where? was my first question.

The book of Exodus is the story of a nation of millions of people who were slaves to another nation. I immediately identified with the word *slave* because I had become addicted to a false god that was destroying my life. This filled my life with all the misery of a slave. My freedom and my loved ones had been cut out of my life, and with my addiction there was an ever increasing desire for an ever diminishing pleasure. I was sinking in spiritual and emotional quicksand. The more I struggled to get out, the faster it sucked me in. I had a desperate need to find my way out, and I found that exit in God's Word.

I started to read in the book of Exodus how the nation of Israel had been enslaved by the nation of Egypt. However, while they were slaves, they enjoyed an enormous advantage uncommon to most slaves: God was on their side, and he demanded that they be set free. After a painful struggle, the slaves finally left the land of their bondage and headed for a place God called "the Promised Land." They went straight to this land and lived happily ever after, right? Wrong! They seemingly were led by God into a trap.

The nation of Israel was confronted

by a large body of water called the Red Sea. With the Egyptian army hot on their trail, it did not look hopeful for the Israelites.

As I read Exodus, I was going through my own period of slavery, and the words of the story shot into my heart. I was reading about my life. I had once believed in God's freedom, yet here I was again a slave. It hadn't yet dawned on me that God might have a purpose in all this. It just seemed as though once again he had let me down. But on further reflection, it was obvious that I had let *him* down. I was forced, as were the Israelites, to figure out the meaning of "God is nowhere." Eventually, I saw a different set of words: God is now here. What a revelation. For the first time I knew I was on my way out, trapped no more by my negative thinking.

So God, according to biblical history, cut a path of dry land through the water — after a few frightening, sleepless nights for the children of Israel, I'm sure. They then moved through the waters to the other side. Standing on the far hillsides, they watched the entire Egyptian army move through the same passageway. Then, the waters closed in and the entire army of Egypt was destroyed. For the first time in the Bible, singing is mentioned as God's people rejoiced and sang a new song unto the Lord.

Sometimes God chooses to lead us into a trap. His plan is to teach us that obstacles can become opportunities. Often we are not moving into an area of growth unless we are dealing with problems that appear unsolvable. This was true for the nation of Israel in their exodus from Egypt. God was preparing to teach them that their problem was there not to break them but to make them. Should we expect it to be any different for God's reluctant servants today?

The poet Annie Johnston Flint wrote:

Have you come to the Red Sea
    place in your life
Where in spite of all you can do
There is no way out, there is no
    way back
There is no other way but through?

So wait on the Lord, with a trust
    serene
Till the night of your fear is past;

He will send the winds and part
the waves
And you will go through at last.

What is the tie between the fright-
ened girl with the black pebble, the
panic-stricken Israelites trapped by
the sea, and the fearful person who is
waiting to make a big change in his or
her life by reading this book? Simply
put, God wants to replace your fear
with faith. Faith says, "I believe with
God's help that I can reach all the
great goals I desire in my heart." Can
you? Sure you can. Who put those
great desires in your heart in the first
place? God did! I hope you'll join me
in saying, "I love you, Lord, for all the
good things you bring out in me. I
thank you."

You are now learning how to

change your tomorrows, and you are doing it by making new, better-informed choices today. For you — and your vision of a whole new world where you no longer live in fear — I stand and applaud!

4 -Trapped by Seething Anger
. . . Up Until Now

Beneath all depression lurks the demon anger.

Andrew Carliss

"Sticks and stones may break my bones, but names will never hurt me." Don't you believe it! Being called names, either as children or as adults, does hurt. It can cut deeply, with scars remaining for a lifetime. The anger might be latent, but it's still there, and there's no telling when the vengeance for past wrongs will surface. Reactive anger traps people into hurting everything or everyone around them in the home, in the office, on the playground, or on a congested freeway. Anger hurts. Anger damages. Anger even kills. But what is anger, and why is it so difficult for us to control? Do we even *want* to control it? Is it part of our emotional makeup from which we have no escape? What can we do to reduce this force in our lives that has hurt us, and others, so much during our lifetime? Must we stay trapped with this *beast that lives within* for the rest of our lives?

Simply put, this hurtful, angry energy we blast out at others stems most often from a deep feeling of hostility toward ourselves. An indecisive, internal civil war between love, which moves us forward, and fear, which moves us backward, leaves us frustrated, feeling our only response is to move against ourselves. Such unstructured anger is like a screaming shell launched in the heat of battle. Having hit its intended target, it continues to spray its shrapnel of death at everything and everyone in the area, including those we most love. This killing fallout often takes the form of accusing others of the very thing we feel about ourselves. Psychologists call this "projected" anger.

How Do You Start Your Day?

Emotionally healthy people tend to awaken each day saying, "Good morning, Lord. It's another good day. Nothing can happen that you and I can't handle together." Others awaken with the gripe, "Good Lord, it's morning. Another lousy day of trying to handle all the stuff that others are going to try to put on me." These are two self-fulfilling prophecies that set the mood and the results for the next sixteen hours. One is content with God's goodness and grace; the other angrily questions whether the Almighty is even remotely involved in the business of the day.

In my experience, most people do not realize how trapped they are in unresolved anger. Recently, I reviewed the results of a psychological test with a woman who'd been seeing me for several weeks. As I went over her responses to several questions, I asked her what she thought might be making her so angry. With a beatific smile spread across a stunned countenance, she straightened up in her chair and responded, "Please, Dr. Freed. I really don't see myself as an angry person, nor would any of my friends. You can just ask them. They'll tell you I'm *not* an angry woman!

Her heart rate accelerated;
her blood pressure rose;
her nose flared;
her face became flushed.
But no, she wasn't angry.

Realizing that my line of questioning would get me nowhere, I waited for a moment to ask casually, "Tell me, what are some of the things that seem to really frustrate you?" For a solid five minutes, denied anger poured from her lips, bordering at

times on rage. Her heart rate accelerated; her blood pressure rose; her
nose flared; her face became flushed.
But no, she wasn't angry. Just frustrated. A little upset. But as she
ranted and raved and stomped
around my office, I understood what
she was saying. That's because I've
been there, as I'm sure you have, so
many times in the past. *No, I'm not
angry. Okay, a little upset, maybe.
But angry? Me? Not on your life.*

I can actually remember the day
when I learned to deny my anger. It
was in a Sunday school class when I
was a little boy in my hometown of
Washington, D.C. One of my buddies had raised his hand that early
Sunday morning and asked, "Teacher,
it seems to me that Jesus got angry
sometimes. He seemed not to like the

way people did some things. He really got mad, didn't he?"

In an attempt to correct what the teacher believed to be theology-gone-wrong, the teacher said something that muddled my mind for many years to come. He replied, "Of course not. Jesus didn't get angry. He couldn't have been angry. He was God's Son. Angry? Never. He just had righteous indignation and perhaps was a little frustrated." The message for that class of boys? Since Jesus was not human enough to become angry over his own life's challenges, then neither should we, if we were to be good Christians, ever admit to an emotion called anger. It would just not be right. It would certainly not be Christian.

Have you been there? If you have,

then you know what I'm talking about. Perhaps like me, the denial of anger may have steered you off into a desert of confusion for much of your life. I remember going home from Sunday school that morning thinking how "frustrated" so many people must be in their lives — friends, teachers, classmates, parents. *Especially* my parents. But thank God I now had learned they weren't angry with me. They were just upset a lot. Bothered. And maybe a little frustrated. This mixed message was all the more disruptive because its falsehood had been reinforced in a context of learning about God.

Anger: The Good and the Bad

At this juncture we need to spell out in more detail the critical difference between reactive and constructive anger. Carol Tavris, in her classic book *Anger*, expresses it as well as anyone when she writes,

Anger, like love, is a moral emotion. It has such a potent capacity for good and evil. I have watched people use anger in the name of emotional liberation to erode affection and trust, whittle away their spirits in bitterness and revenge, and diminish their dignity in years of spiteful hatred. And I watch with admiration those who use anger to probe for truth, who challenge and change the complacent injustices of life, and who take an unpopular position center stage while others say "Shhh" from the wings. In the last several decades, biology and psychology have deprived anger, and our other emotions, of the human capacity for choice and control. My aim here, in evaluating and criticizing the prevailing wisdom, is to help to restore confidence in these human gifts.

Amazing. Tavris calls anger, and our other emotions, gifts, which is what they truly are. We *are* our emotions, and our emotions *are* us. She implies that reactive anger is a habit of the mind in that it encourages the voice to speak before engaging the brain. Would you not agree that most of our anger problems arise from talking before thinking? This is why the old saying speaks of counting to ten. Biblical wisdom says that "a wise man thinks ahead" (Proverbs 13:16, TLB). Today we speak of this as being proactive, constructive, the kind of "anger maintenance" that brings together disparate hearts and emotions, rather than seeing them cast each other aside.

God's Word Has the Answer

When you and I accept God's eternal truth as the standard for our lives, we no longer are obliged to react with our old, outdated, uninformed anger to the malice and discontent that surround us.

When you and I feel trapped by our anger, the reactive kind, we need a biblically based, proactive boundary to get us out of our emotional tailspin. This is essentially the counsel we read in Paul's letter to the Roman church, where he tells the Christians at Rome:

> Don't let the world around you squeeze you into its own mold, but let God remold your minds from within, so that you may prove in practice that the plan of God for you is good, meets all his demands and moves toward the goal of true maturity.
> (Romans 12:2, PHILLIPS)

Here's the good news in this passage: We now operate on a different wavelength. Now we see that the cause is from within us and the effect is out there. We've made a conscious decision, with God's help, to no longer let the world around us squeeze us into its *status quo*. The writer of Proverbs agrees:

A man who lacks judgment de-
rides his neighbor, but a man of
understanding holds his tongue.
(Proverbs 11:12)

He who guards his lips guards his
life, but he who speaks rashly will
come to ruin.
(Proverbs 13:3)

The apostle Paul then gives us one
of the most sound pieces of advice
we'll ever hear when he writes to the
church at Ephesus, "If you are angry,
be sure that it is not out of wounded
pride or bad temper. Never go to bed
angry — don't give the devil that sort
of foothold" (Ephesians 4:26–27,
PHILLIPS).

The above Scripture tells us that between the stimulus and the response of anger there is a space to ask some important questions, such as *Will how I'm about to react help me get what I truly want? If I choose impulsive, angry words, I realize I may feel good, even justified, but will it be worth the pain and regret to come?* Since you and I know what our answers will be, we will certainly choose the kinds of quiet words that turn away wrath, that keep relationships intact and bring peace to our troubled hearts. When we do this, we can say, "Thank you, Lord. You've taken me out of the trap, and to you I'm eternally grateful."

Victims No More

Why is it so important to answer the

above questions correctly? Because if you and I choose to let others make us angry, then we choose the life of a victim. We keep on reinforcing that person's perverse need to push our buttons. This gives someone else the power to throw us out of control. Why would we do that? Why would we give someone else the control button to make us sound like uncivil, blathering idiots?

In all honesty, up until now you may have played the role of victim. Isn't it good news that you do not need to respond that way anymore? The next time someone inappropriately rings the doorbell of your emotions, you will be strong and will respond, not in kind, but with kindness. That is what is meant by the advice *not to let the world around us squeeze us into its mold.* Spiritually, physically and emotionally, *it's the only way to live.*

What we must note here is that anger is a reach for power and control. But self-esteem also requires power and control to enhance and protect its feelings of peace and well-being. So the problem is obviously *not* power and control but what we *do* with this enormous twin energy force that can be used equally for good and for ill. The next time you feel hurt emotionally by someone's verbal attacks, respond by saying, "I won't allow you to keep yelling at me like that anymore. That also goes for insults, criticism and humiliation. All that must come to an end. And if, for some reason, you continue to attack me, I will walk away."

Having said this, there is still an un-answered question about our entrapment and anger. The question is this: Who is trapping whom? The Bible knows you and me so well that it continually reminds us that a savage battle within us continues unabated. Romans 7 speaks of this inner war as the *shoulds* we don't do and the *shouldn'ts* we do. It's fascinating how the words of the apostle Paul speak as strongly to us today as they did almost two thousand years ago. On one occasion Paul spoke of his own challenges when he penned the words, "Don't get all tied up again in the chains of slavery" (Galatians 5:1, TLB). Slavery indeed. That's what being trapped is all about, and unresolved anger is the most terrible captor of all.

A Hostility Check

Dr. Redford Brown Williams, author of *Anger Kills*, has devised a simple checklist for us to use to check our "hostility level." You may find the following quiz of interest as you work through whatever may be angering you.

1. Are you generally mistrustful and cynical? For example, do you frequently check up on a partner's performance or point out how something could be done better?

2. Do you secretly think most people are stupid or pathetic, deserving whatever happens to them?

3. Do you get very angry if someone disrupts your daily routine, say, by leaving the newspaper scattered around so you can't read it easily

or forgetting to buy milk for your coffee?

4. If someone at work offers to help you with a task, do you feel angry because they think you are not smart enough to do it alone?

5. Do you honk your horn repeatedly when the car in front of you doesn't move quickly after the light turns green?

TAKE ACTION

Dr. Williams suggests that if you answer yes to any of these questions you might want to start keeping a diary of daily irritations, cynical thoughts and hostile feelings. It should be detailed enough to give you a clear picture of how often — and why — you become upset, as well as how you typically respond. If what is bothering you seems unimportant, let it go. Or if your frustration is about things beyond your ability to change, again, just let it go. Before long, you'll discover how unproductive it is to upset yourself with angry thoughts.

Some situations, however, merit constructive anger. A twenty-something woman I'll call Sarah sat in my office and told me her mother had phoned three times in the past two weeks, saying, "Honey, I just happened to drive by your house again last night and noticed the babysitter's car was still there at midnight. You know, I really think you shouldn't be leaving my granddaughter with a babysitter so often." Imagine the feelings of the young mother. She was livid, and her anger started to build.

Sarah told me, "Dr. Freed, one day Mother called me, and I got so frustrated with what she was saying that I just put the receiver on the table and walked around the house for ten minutes just to cool off. When I picked it up again ten minutes later, Mother was still on the line, telling me how to raise my kids. She didn't even know I hadn't been listening to her!"

After Sarah and I talked about her dilemma, we had a little strategy session on how she might best work through her problem. The first thing she did when she went home was to call her mother and invite her to lunch. A few days later, mother and daughter were seated at a restaurant. Even before the entree arrived, Sarah said, "Mom, I want our relationship to be different. I'm giving you an A for motherhood, but now I would like to graduate you to the status of *friend*. Just be my friend."

With that, her mother started stuttering and stammering. "What on earth are you talking about, Sarah? I'm already your friend."

Sarah responded, "Mother, friends don't tell one another how to live their lives. Be my friend. Build me up. Love looks for ways to be constructive. Don't put me down for not mothering as you did. Remember how you disliked your mother's doing that to you, Mom? Please, just be my friend."

In tears, her mother began to understand, and today Sarah and her mother are the best of friends. Trapped no more by anger, Sarah finally crossed the threshold to an exciting, new life for herself with the ones she loved.

Four Ways to Deal with Anger

Let's look at some options in the management of our anger. We've already alluded to them, but now let's look at each one specifically. There are essentially four ways to work through the anger that has you trapped and immobilized: *repress it, suppress it, express it* or *confess it.*

1. *Repressing* an angry feeling traps you in it so deeply that through a well-orchestrated program of denial you don't even realize you have the emotion. Perhaps an authority figure told you at an early age that "you shouldn't have angry feelings." As a result, you

may now feel afraid, embarrassed, and even angrier, with less ability to deal with your denied emotions. The main challenge with repressing your feelings is that you can never bury them *dead*. They are very much alive, wriggling about, kicking up their heels and refusing to keel over. In your always futile attempts to bury them, you have merely thrown a few shovelfuls of dirt over what you thought were emotional cadavers, hoping you'd never hear from them again. A grave mistake. Repressed feelings of anger will stay with you, trouble you and undermine you until you face them. Then you can choose to release them with a person you trust.

2. *Suppressing* angry feelings

means you are constantly fighting them with ill-equipped, worn-out *shoulds* and *shouldn'ts*. When you trap yourself by suppressing your anger, you become immobilized with anxiety compounded by other closely kept secrets (suppressed emotions) that eat away at your emotional core. Freud was correct when he suggested, "Your secrets are your sickness." When you suppress your feelings of anger, you almost never get what you want. You just want to go along and get along. You don't rock the boat. You hold your anger inside. You risk turning your feelings into physical illnesses as, in the process of denial, you set yourself up for a backache, headache, neckache, peptic ulcer or any other number of physical ailments.

So the question: what *shoulds* are you putting on yourself right now? Are you still trapped by saying, *I should take the abuse of others; I should just be a sitting duck for others to shoot at.* I hope not. The word *should* discourages; the word *can* encourages. Once you release yourself from the guilt of your own *shoulds,* you can move assertively in an emotionally healthy direction, finally becoming the person God designed you to be. In that process, you'll discover that the three most powerful motivating phrases to help you produce lasting change are: *I can, I will* and *I do.*

3. For some people, *expressing* a

feeling means blowing up in anger and letting it all hang out. For years, many therapists encouraged their clients to "let your anger fly . . . just let it out . . . It'll do you good." We now know this is not a healthy response, but rather one that leaves indelible scars and hurts. It *does* matter who stands in the path of our anger. It *does* matter what we say, how we say it and when we say it. If the anger (that arises out of hurt, fear and frustration) is not expressed in an environment where it can be talked out and understood, how can we justify bringing out the verbal guns and blasting our target into relational oblivion? It's been said that a person is about as big as the things that make him or her angry. Perhaps better said, the more you grow up, the less you will blow up.

If you don't talk your angry feelings out with someone, you will take <u>them out on someone.</u>

4. *Confessing* a feeling means learning to agree to talk it out. If you don't talk your angry feelings out *with* someone, you will take them out *on* someone. Initially, you may be fearful in taking this step toward emotional well-being, and that's understandable. But once you learn to talk out these feelings a little at a time, you will find a release from the trap you've lived in for too long. For example, right now, as you read this chap-

ter, you may be feeling sad, re-jected, uncared for, unappreci-ated, even emotionally abused. If so, I want you to find someone you trust to talk to. Ask this person just to sit with you and listen to you. You don't need a psychology text filled with edu-cated answers for solace, nor do you need to take an exhaustive personality inventory. You simply need someone who will *hang in there* with you as you share your deepest feelings.

TAKE ACTION

If you *repress* your feelings of anger, you run the risk of burying other feelings alive. If you *suppress* them with a parade of *shoulds,* you will heap guilt on yourself and may never achieve the emotional health God created you to enjoy. If you *express* your feelings with anger and hostility, you might feel justified for a while. However, you will leave a trail of emotionally battered bodies and shattered relationships along the way, some of which may never recover. But when you are able to *confess* and share the pain and frustration that's in your heart with a loving, listening, nonjudgmental person, you will begin to feel peace within yourself.

I hope you better understand the role that anger has played in your life to keep you trapped . . . up until now. Will those around you this coming week feel that you are less angry than before? If you choose to be, you will be, and you will be free at last, on your way out of the trap of anger and despair. I want that very much for you right now.

5 -Trapped by Sexual Needs
. . . Up Until Now

Illicit sex is the effort of the flesh to rape the spirit. Only spiritual strength can resist this attack.

Alfred Gross

Nancy was fifteen years old and very pregnant. She sat before me crying as she talked about her first sexual encounter six months earlier. She believed the lie of helplessness; she said she was not able to say no to the boy. I suggested she might have said, "I'm just not ready for that."

Immediately she blurted, "Gee,

that's the way I was really feeling. I wish I'd known how to say that at the time. I think that might have worked."

So many things don't seem to work out right with our strong sexual feelings — situations that plague men, women, boys and girls within the church as much as anyone else. Sexual feelings are no respecter of a person's gender, age, racial origin or station in life. They are there with us, and we must deal with them at all times. In this chapter we're going to look at what we do with our sexual feelings as single people and married ones.

We Live in an Age of Myths

Myths are the lies that we tell ourselves, the devices that help us deny truth until we are finally confronted with it. Unfortunately, when the truth hits, it usually comes as a battering ram, knocking down our most fortified structures, and reminding us in an instant that we are frail. There are many myths in our society surrounding sex outside of marriage. Let's look at some of these.

Myth One: We're just not quite ready to make a total commitment, but we love each other, so sex is okay. It will only be a matter of time until we get married.

Fact: Today's statistics overwhelmingly indicate that premarital sex or living together is not the prelude to a happy marriage.

Myth Two: You can't really get to

know a person until you have lived together and known each other in bed.

Fact: Actually, people who live together are inclined to get to know each other's faults. Yet far from leading couples to a more realistic view of marriage, living together tends to reinforce the myth that "he/she will change after we're married." But those faults don't go away, and the trap of wishful thinking holds the spouses even more tightly. Further, the naughty, secret sex that two people engage in before marriage immediately changes after marriage. Without the excitement of breaking the rules, sex can be much less interesting to those who don't know how to make it good.

Myth Three: We're madly in love and trust each other totally. We don't need marriage.

Fact: The odds are overwhelming that one of the partners will gradually become *more* emotionally invested as the other becomes *less.*

For many people sex outside of marriage is just a lifestyle choice. Two consenting teens or adults, if they take precautions, can have sex without any negative consequences. Besides, some people reason, the Bible forbade fornication because there was no way to prevent pregnancy. But that's no longer true. Does this mean that the commitment to marriage can now be replaced with a promise to live together for a while? *Shacking up* would be one contemporary term for this living arrangement.

A five-page article in *Cosmopolitan*, October 1976, was titled "Living Together Is a Rotten Idea." Check out this first paragraph of the article. As you do, try to restrain yourself from saying that it was written almost three decades ago and is therefore now outdated beyond reason. My experience as a counselor suggests that it is not.

When a woman lives with a man without the couple making the mutual and wholehearted investment of themselves backed by a marriage certificate, she immediately loses the following things: her independence; her freedom to make her own choices; her privacy; all of her mystery; any of her practical bargaining position in the power-structure of love; an opportunity to make a meaningful change in her life by taking a genuine step toward full adult status; the prospect of having a child other than an illegitimate one; and the protection of the law. [This same paragraph could be written for a man.]

For many it will be easy to dismiss the forgoing as being outdated. Others will resonate with these truths as part of their own up-to-date, late-twentieth-century experience. Could it be possible there actually *are* some universal truths about human relationships? Perhaps you already have encountered some of the myths that surround this now common situation. Nothing is easier than to mistake truth for falsehood, especially when values tend to come from peer pressure, the media and the questionable advice of well-meaning friends.

The More You Fight, the More You Lose

Over the years, many ministers of God have come to me for help in understanding their inner conflicts. During those hundreds of hours of agonizing sessions, they have told me repeatedly, "I have fought my sexual feelings all my life, and lost. It seems as though the harder I fight them, the stronger they get." I then explain that this is exactly what will happen until they understand this one important truth: You can never fight a strong feeling without giving it the attention you don't want it to have.

Because they are ministers of the gospel, these men are interested when I open the Bible and show them how God's Word never suggests we deal with our feelings by fighting or suppressing them. On page after page of Scripture, we learn that the harder we push against these feelings, the harder they push back. Usually, at this point, the sincere minister, wanting to get on with his or her life, cries out in desperation: "Then what do I do? The things I shouldn't do, I do, and the things I should do, I don't."

I respond, "Well, you are certainly not alone. In fact, you are in pretty good company because what you've just said is also ably expressed by the apostle Paul, who seemed to be writing while in deep depression. And what did he do?"

The pastor's answer usually comes from the left brain. "Well, I guess he simply changed his attitude about God." This is a breakthrough, because at this point the pastor turns on the lights and feelings about God's presence and power in his life. In doing so, he turns off the struggle with himself and his inability to exercise self-control.

You can never fight a strong feeling without giving it the attention you <u>don't want it to have.</u>

I can then say, "You mean he just

changed his thinking to another channel? Kind of like you'd zap a television set with a remote to go to another program?" The pastor will usually nod in agreement.

Here's the point I want to plant in your heart: You and I will begin to see the world differently when we think differently about what we want to see.

But I Have These Sexual Feelings

But, as some will say, it doesn't work that way. You wish it would, but it's not that easy. Are you saying your biggest worry is that you cannot *stop* your sexual feelings? Please listen carefully. Did anyone ask you to *stop* having them? Why would you want to kill off those vital feelings that God created in you and called good?

Jesus taught that he who looks on a woman and lusts after her has committed adultery in his heart. Does that mean that sexual thoughts and the act of adultery are one and the same? No. Adultery is a systematic plan to seduce another person sexually for one's own selfish pleasure. That's a planned sexual agenda, not a sexual thought.

We now come to that thin line between chosen thoughts and compulsive thinking. When we cross this line, we no longer choose the thoughts. The thoughts now have chosen us. We are addicted.

In sexual thinking, a person can choose from many possible pathways of thought. With a healthy family background of loving affirmation and straightforward information, sex as a beautiful gift of God can be embraced in many life-enhancing ways. By contrast, a background of sexual abuse and disinformation in a dysfunctional family setting can make one's sexuality a curse, leading into the horrifying trap of addiction. Patrick Carnes, a national authority on addictive sexuality, states in his book *Out of the Shadows*:

A common definition of alcoholism is that a person has a pathological relationship with a mood-altering chemical. This relationship with alcohol becomes more important than family, friends and work. . . . The sexual addiction is parallel. The addict's relationship with a mood-altering experience becomes central to his life.

Carnes goes on to write about this in a way that makes it sound like a spiritual experience with God. In fact, it is such an experience — with a false god. Carnes observes that the sexual experience is the source of nurturing, the focus of energy, and the origin of excitement. It is the remedy for pain and anxiety, the reward for success, and the means for maintaining emotional balance.

A client of mine, Mike, was a sophomore in college who had served in the Navy for four years before starting school. He came into therapy with me with this presenting problem: "I have difficulty studying, my grades are bad, and I think I have Attention Deficit Disorder."

Along with this on his intake chart was Mike's answer to a question about his use of alcohol. He checked the moderate-usage box and explained this as "one or two beers a day." Under religious affiliation he wrote, "Baptist," and the person he wanted contacted in case of emergency was his girlfriend Nancy.

In our first session, he told me, among other things, that he no longer attended church and that he had sex every Wednesday night with Nancy. Mental red flags arose for me due to his clearly defined amount of beer and sex.

Prior to our second session, Michael took a computerized test that indicated that attention deficit was unlikely. When we met again, I asked Mike if there was anything in his life he was pretending not to know. He asked, "Like what?"

I responded, "Like any secrets you might be keeping from everybody, and from me." I then explained his right to confidentiality. Over the next four sessions Mike's story gradually unfolded.

Mike had been sexually abused by his grandfather over a period of three years when he was six to nine years old. This occurred every Wednesday when his parents were at the church prayer meeting. His grandfather gave him some money and made him promise each time never to tell anyone about their relationship.

As Mike finished describing this relationship, he blurted out, "Here I am telling you the whole thing. I'll probably end up telling you, too, that I'm always thinking about my next opportunity to be with a woman." He went on to say that Nancy wasn't the only girl in his life and that he was always finding new women to have sex with. When asked how this made him feel, he responded, "Sex makes me feel good about myself, even better than when I became a Christian. Then I couldn't be what I was supposed to be, and now I'm always on the prowl getting what I have to get. . . . Actually," he continued, "this is a rotten way to live, and most of the time I really feel like a rotten guy."

Finally, I asked him what the fuel was for his prowling.

"You mean my desire?" he asked.

"No, I mean your alcohol consumption," I responded.

"I only drink a few six-packs a day," he admitted.

So Mike was diagnosed with both sexual and alcohol addiction. This is not uncommon, as the latter paves the way for the former. Later on, Michael described himself as "worshiping at the shrine of alcohol and sex." He boasted that these were his "higher power" and that he learned this at an AA meeting. I tried to talk to him about the Prodigal Son story described in the Bible, but he could not relate to my thoughts.

Michael never came back to me after that. The notes of my last session ended with the words: "Next week talk about Overcomers Outreach." I never had the chance to do that. Michael's story reminds me of a similar account told by Leo Buscaglia in *Living, Loving and Learning*. He reports reading a letter from a college coed that went something like this:

Remember the time I borrowed your brand-new car and I dented it? I thought you would strangle me, but you didn't.

Remember the time I dragged you to the beach and you didn't want to go? You said it would rain, and it did. I thought you would say, "I told you so," but you didn't.

Remember the time I spilled blueberry pie on your new car rug? I thought you would kill me, but you didn't.

And remember the time you took me out and I thought I was so cute and flirted with all the guys and you got jealous? I thought you would drop me, but you didn't.

Remember the time I invited you to the dance and I forgot to tell you that it was formal and you showed up in your Levis? I thought you would leave me, but you didn't.

Yes, there were lots of things you didn't do, but you put up with me and protected me and loved me, and I never told you how much I appreciated it. I was going to make that all up to you when you got back from Vietnam, but you didn't.

TAKE ACTION
Neither Mike nor this soldier had

the opportunity to hear what they really needed. But to those of you reading this book who are trapped in alcohol or sexual addiction, I do have the chance to tell you about Overcomers Outreach. This is a group of Christian men and women who have banded together in recovery from addictions through a twelve-step program set in a Christian context. This is a national networking group that receives referrals from such ministries as the 700 Club, Focus on the Family (which has an Overcomers group on its premises), and the Billy Graham Evangelistic Association. Staff members receive calls from all over the country, and there are now close to a thousand Overcomers Outreach groups in nearly every state, as well as in ten foreign countries. They will understand where you are coming from when you call. Their phone number is (800) 310-3001. Their e-mail is info@overcomersoutreach.org. Their address is P.O. Box 2208, Oakhurst, CA 93644. Their Web site is www.overcomersoutreach.org. They say that they bridge the gap between traditional twelve-step support groups and hurting people in churches of all denominations. If you need them, they are ready to give you hope and help.

6 -Trapped in a Non-Intimate Marriage
. . . *Up Until Now*

True intimacy with another human being can only be experienced when you have found true peace within yourself.

Angela L. Wozniak

The most basic truth about a marital relationship is that *it is always growing*. It is either growing closer together or growing further apart. It is never static. So what are the key components of a healthy marriage? What sets it apart and moves it away from the realm of the mediocre and the common?

In a healthy marriage, not only are two people growing closer, which could happen as a result of any crisis, fear or for any number of other reasons, but they also are continually seeking greater intimacy with each other. They are going for each other's heart, and for starters, each partner first checks up on his or her own heart by asking certain questions, such as, *What words of encouragement have I spoken today? What acts of kindness do I continually perform for the one I love? How am I demonstrating a more loving me? Is what I am about to do with or for my beloved bringing us closer together or driving us further apart?* With this deep introspection comes the even deeper awareness that the greatest need of the human heart is to be affirmed, and to be affirmed often. In many cases, this outpouring of love for another results from an even greater, more powerful inpouring of God's love as demonstrated through the love of Christ. What we put in is what we will put out. Garbage in, garbage out. Love in, love out.

Because I am loved, I am loving, and because I am loving, I am loved.

Roget's Thesaurus has gathered hundreds of words on the subject of intimacy, such as *nearness, closeness, openness, touching.* The mental picture is of two people who enjoy each other, walking side by side, hand in hand, listening intently to one another, loving each other un-ashamedly. Keep that picture in your mind. Then redefine your definition of intimacy as "the enjoyment of the full compatibility of mind and heart."

I think you would agree that while there are many intimacies in a marital relationship, some always seem to stand out as major factors. I would like to suggest what I think are the *six basic intimacies* that are critical to a healthy, intimate relationship: *emotional, financial, intellectual, recreational, sexual and spiritual* intimacies. Since these intimacies vary for many people in their hierarchy of importance, I've listed them alphabetically. Now, however, as I look at the list, I'm somewhat concerned to see *spiritual intimacy* bringing up the rear. For many of us, this is the intimacy where a loving God helps teach us all the other loving ways we need to relate to those who are our partners for life. The fact that spiritual intimacy is last on the list does not mean it is the least in importance. We'll talk more about this later. As you read the following, I want you to ponder the importance of each intimacy in your life, then give yourself a score of A, B, C, D or F as it relates to your marriage. The more honest you are in your evaluation, the more you will be helped by what you are about to read.

1. Emotional Intimacy

Emotional intimacy means getting in touch with your feelings. It goes beyond the "How are you . . . I'm fine" routine of casual conversation.

It picks up on the present, inner state of your being. It always results from what you've been thinking. For example, right now I'm feeling excited about writing these words for you to understand. How much I wish I'd known these things earlier in my own life. A lot of health could have been gained and a lot of my hurt avoided.

Now I'm feeling exhilarated in being able to share with you some of the truths that have made my life so much happier. I am confident they will do the same for you. So, I've just shared my feelings of being excited and happy to be with you in this moment. Now what are you feeling as you read this? Isn't there a deeper relationship building between us? If I could call you by your first name and say, "_____, I'm so excited and happy that we've met," couldn't you feel the pleasure?

Let's say you've just been on your first date with Sue or with John. If both of you had shared pleasurable feelings like this, wouldn't there be a second date? The expression of the feelings of your heart enables you and others to share in a richer quality of life. This is what *relating* is all about. It is finding your self as the real *you* and opening something up — *your heart*. Feelings are heart talk, and they are contagious. They are caught by the heart of another, and in the process these two hearts can merge and beat as one.

Relating is finding the real you and opening something up — your heart.

Relating requires two people opening themselves to each other. But
some people have a misimpression
about what it means to become one.
When was the last time you went to a
wedding, perhaps your own, where
three candles stood at the front of the
beautifully decorated church? The
center candle was unlighted. Then, at
a planned moment in the ceremony,
the bride and groom stood together
to light the central candle, signifying
that the two had now become one —
one as a couple, and one in Christ.
What a warm feeling flowed throughout the crowd of supporters. Just recently I observed this, but what happened next in the ceremony made me
feel bad. The couple blew out their
candles! I wanted to cry out, "No,
don't do that!"

TAKE ACTION

You have to keep your own flame and regularly touch it to the eternal flame of God, otherwise your candle is going to burn out. Keep the fire going, to touch each other daily with the warm feelings of your hearts.

In reading this you may be saying, "Come on now, this may happen once in a while, but you just can't always have warm feelings. What happens when your feelings are cold, negative and potentially hurtful toward one another, even toward the one you say you love most?" This question is of great importance, and we will answer it in the upcoming chapters.

2. Financial Intimacy

Financial intimacy touches a sensitive nerve, doesn't it? Who has not had problems with money — how to spend it, save it or give it away? Financial intimacy has to do with one's view of monetary power and how it is to be used. Since money *is* power, then money can corrupt, and absolute money power has the ability to corrupt absolutely. A person with great financial assets feels that anything can be bought. Now before you say, "but it can't buy people," I want to say "it can especially buy people." At this point our value systems become threatened almost beyond belief. We could go far afield with this, so let's avoid that tendency and target some areas that create traps of financial intimacy for couples.

One area of concern is credit cards; the other has to do with gratification, instant or delayed. There can be no financial feelings of good will in a relationship of a spender and a saver. At the earliest opportunity in a relationship, check out the compatibility here. Trouble is brewing if one who has been scrimping and saving for a rainy day learns that the loved one has five maxed-out credit cards being paid off at huge interest rates and is looking for still more credit for the things he or she needs "right now." The only way not to see disaster here would be for the two to be so otherwise bonded that they have become blind to the incompatibilities. This often happens when sex is the first intimacy of bonding. "Little" things such as money problems seem small. However, sooner or later these "small problems" will threaten the relationship's very existence.

It's true that *opposites attract*. But opposing views on money are destructive and frequently nonnegotiable in a relationship. Disagreements on how to use money may be only the beginning of a litany of other problems. Why would opposite views on a lot of things be attractive for some one who is seeking a good relationship? Surely you can learn to accept *in love* the other person's differences. But isn't it more sensible to enjoy and celebrate in love the other person's similarities? Why do the conventions and large events we attend appeal to us? Is it not a commonality of interest and attitude? I realize there are differing opinions on virtually any subject, but is it more satisfying to be with people who are more *like* you or *unlike* you? Financial stability and a common approach to spending and saving is vital to any relationship. If you are trapped in this area, I encourage you to seek help now. You can say you are trapped, but you also have the choice to add "up until now."

TAKE ACTION

I hope you can say to your beloved what I say to my darling wife, "The things in me I like to be are the things in you I like to see." How are you doing in the financial intimacy department? What kind of grade do you give yourself? Whatever your mark, this might be a good time to go back to school.

3. Intellectual Intimacy

The intellectual bonding of two minds means you have great respect for the way the other person thinks. The very fact that he was smart enough to choose you should be good for your ego, and the reverse logic is true for his. Few things can do more damage to a relationship than to imply or call the other person *stupid* or *incompetent*. This means that your partner has made some dumb choices, and you may have been one of them. To say, "That's stupid" is really to say, "You're stupid." This is so opposite to the way of love, which looks for the best in another and strives, works hard at, finding ways to be constructive.

> "The meaning of your communication is the response you elicit." Tony Robbins

To say to someone, "You have a great mind, even though we disagree on this issue" is a much better way to go. But let's take it a bit further. Try this: We each have great minds. Now let's use our minds to figure out why we disagree on this matter. Then *together* you can search out a new discovery and come to a meeting of both your minds. Intellectual intimacy has to do with a feeling of shared equity. Let's listen to a comment I often hear in the premarital counseling I do. This comes in answer to my question: Do either of you feel intellectually inferior or superior to the other?

I frequently get this response, often

from the man: "Well, I have a college degree, *but she's the reader*." What does that statement mean? Is it arrogant? I don't think so. Is it loving? I'd think quite likely. Is it revealing? You bet it is. Isn't this person implying, knowingly or not, that he was a reader in the past and she is a reader in the present? Anything wrong with this?

One of today's outstanding writers and thinkers on the art of communication is Tony Robbins. He brilliantly observes that "the meaning of your communication is the response you elicit." In the above context, intimacy is enhanced if the woman honestly replies: "That's no problem. After I come home from work, I like to read. When he comes home, he likes to watch TV. I've got no problem with that." Will this create difficulties later on? Probably not, as long as neither gets judgmental over the other's behavior.

If the husband, on the other hand, speaks defensively about his wife's reading, then the couple can know there is a miscommunication. It means that for some reason he is hearing her criticizing him for not reading. If that happens, then she will enhance their intimacy if she can assure him of her acceptance. And he would do well to examine his reasons for feeling put down. Here's the key thought in this situation: When the response turns reactive and defensive, let the first communicator look for the *should* or *shouldn't* that may have been heard in what was said.

4. Recreational Intimacy

Recently I suggested to a couple with a troubled marriage that they needed to lighten up and start enjoying each other. The look in their eyes told me they hadn't the foggiest idea of how to do this. I asked what they enjoyed doing together in the early days of their courtship. All they could come up with was eating out together. I gave it one more shot. "Well, surely you enjoyed talking together." Their response was, "No, we have never talked much, not at the beginning, and not now." One does not need to be a counselor to know that their marriage already was trapped.

Your relational problems might be small by comparison. I believe most couples remember times when they truly enjoyed each other. That's why you and you beloved kept seeing each other day after day, weekend after weekend. You loved being together. There was a synergy about your togetherness that magnified the good feelings about being alive. You loved the times you skied down the slopes together or played paddleball on a sandy beach. The movies you talked about added excitement to your life, and all those baseball and football games made hot dogs and peanuts taste so good. And then there were the holidays. You had fun with each other's families. Those were the good old days. But what happened to them? Where are they now? Why are they no longer in your schedule of events? It's at this point I often hear the saddest words of all, "Well, we used to enjoy all that, but then the kids came along. . . ."

Perhaps a conversation I had with two people (I'll call them Bill and Susan) will say it best. Susan began by saying the familiar phrase, "Well, we used to enjoy all that, but then the kids came along. Things happened that it seems we weren't prepared for. First, we stopped being a carefree couple, and we took on the title of *parents*. Yes, it was exciting, but I got so involved with that little life forming in me. I'd talk to her, I wanted a girl, and would come up with huge lists of names, always searching for that one name that would suit her perfectly. Then I would feel her kick. Wow! I'd put Bill's hand on my stomach and let him feel her movements."

When I asked Bill how he felt about this, he said, "I thought it was great and . . ."

"Bill, I asked you how you FELT about this."

"Well, I think I was very happy."

"Bill, tell me how you really felt."

Long pause. "Well, actually . . . I felt so left out, as if I were on the outside looking in. Like something was changing and it didn't feel good."

"What was changing, Bill?"

Love is always something you do.

Silence. "I hate to say this. I didn't even realize it at first, but I was feeling angry about something, very angry. I felt as if things would never be the same again, and it just now dawns on me what it was. I would never be number one again in Susan's life. It still feels that way."

Hearing this, I wondered if Susan would become belligerent in her communication with her husband, saying perhaps, "Bill, that's not true. It was never true. I always loved you, and I always saw you as number one." Or would she instead bring back some of those wonderful, playful behaviors that once made Bill know he was number one? I think you can understand which would be better.

TAKE ACTION

The important truth here is that love is always something you do. From the sorry lament of "we used to," you can now respond with "watch me do it again." It can be your loving way to help end the clutter of a busy, distracted life that has buried the fun things you did together. You've taken each other for granted, switched too many of your once-important priorities, and allowed the cares of the world to keep you from enjoying each other's company . . . *up until now*.

5. Sexual Intimacy

For many couples, sexual intimacy at the outset of their relationship becomes the most intense bonding of all. This creates a danger that sexual intimacy will blind them to everything else. Sex can both *bond* a relationship and at the same time *blind* people from seeing the many important missing ingredients. Just six months ago, only a few weeks before they were to be married, a couple — both schoolteachers — came to see me for just one session. I chose to run them, like a quick x-ray, through the "intimacy test." I asked them to give a grade for each of the intimacies in their relationship. They went through with straight A's. This raised enough doubt in my mind about their relationship that I suggested another session. They were too busy. Six months later they were still too busy to see me. He was busy getting a lawyer for a divorce. She was busy trying to figure it all out. She finally chose to come to my office where, with great emotion, she asked me what had gone wrong.

"What do you think?" I asked.

"Well, I remember clearly your

telling us that it is always easier to get into something than to get out of it. But how could we have been so blind? Of all those intimacies for which we gave ourselves straight A's, *not one exists today.* Not a single one."

I asked her which of the intimacies they lost first and in what order they lost the rest.

Her response was so significant: "We lost only two. The fun together died three months ago, and the sex died six weeks ago. The others we thought we had, but we really didn't."

Silence.

"How dumb we were, thinking that fun and sex would be enough to make a good marriage. We really blew it."

In a different scenario, what would

happen to a couple that really does have A's in four out of six of the intimacies? Their report card might look something like this:

Emotional — D
Financial — A
Intellectual — A
Recreational — A
Sexual — D
Spiritual — A

Would you ask them which of the lower grades they need to work on? Would you ask them if they would like to try to raise their emotional and sexual intimacy scores to a C? What would you expect them to say to you? You'd probably hear the man say, "I'd like to raise my sexual intimacy grade to a C." The woman? "I think I would like to change my emotional grade from a D to a C."

What about you? What would your score be on these various areas of <u>intimacy?</u>

Who is answering the right question with the right answer? The woman? Right. People can't have good sex if they are unable to communicate emotionally, including communicate about sex. Where might the strong A in spiritual intimacy come into play? I really don't know. Sometimes people are told from early life that they shouldn't *think* a lot about sex, and for sure they shouldn't *talk* about it.

This couple has been married for five years with two children, yet they still can't talk about sex. Maybe they feel it's dirty and they shouldn't talk about it. But whatever the reason, it makes the spouses vulnerable to being attracted to someone outside the marriage who *is* able to talk about sex. At that point one learns real quick what that A in spirituality really means.

6. *Spiritual Intimacy*

What does this vital component for a healthy relationship really mean? Let's say, for starters, that spirituality has something to do with deep, lasting values and how we perceive our world: Is this a friendly universe or a scary, angry place to be? Maybe if there's a loving God behind the scenes, it is the former; if there is no such kind and compassionate being, then it would surely be the latter. Many of us believe this God communicates with love and grace. This means he cares about us individually. It means God knows our names, our strengths and weaknesses. It means we know that he is God and that we are not. Like the psalmist, we know we are but tiny specks in the universe, yet we are very important tiny specks.

When we tap into true spirituality and rely on the presence, power and potential of a God-who-lives-within, we learn to resolve our conflicts with love and grace. When true spirituality is put into high gear in the lives of two people in love, jangled nerves become soothed. Toxic talk loses its poison. The weak find protection. The bold and the brash discover there is *an-*

other way. Self-esteem is heightened. It is no longer a *reactionship* but a *re-lationship*. As the old song goes, "There is peace in the valley." Lovers start to talk sense to themselves, no longer trying to talk sense into someone else. They find common ground for agreement.

In the Old Testament there are thirty-nine books, beginning with Genesis and ending with Malachi. Both Jewish and Christian believers base their faith on these truths as God's revelation of himself. He is called Jehovah, which is basically the first person singular for the words *I am*. This simply and wonderfully means "he is always in the present tense." Now, we can hold this truth in our head or we can be held by God in our heart.

Those who see God with the eyes of the heart also hear him with the ears of the heart. And this is what we hear — that he is *for* us!

Jehovah Jirah — I am the provision for your need.

Jehovah Rapha — I am the healing for your heart.

Jehovah Hissi — I am the banner (flag) for your allegiance.

Jehovah Rab — I am your shepherd as you join my flock of sheep.

Jehovah Sidbena — I am your righteousness in the forgiveness of your sin.

Authentic spirituality, real and undefiled, is not going to church, attending weekly Bible studies, tithing, singing in the choir, or even witnessing to the reality of our faith, as vital as all these are to Christian growth and a walk with God. These are important behaviors that result from an awareness that the Father loves you so much that he provides for your every need; that he is there with you twenty-four hours a day to heal your hurts of body and mind; that he is your cheerleader, the One who always shows up for you as you play the game of life; that he is your loving, tender Shepherd and the One who will always forgive you every time you step off the path of righteousness. This is where real spirituality begins and ends. When both partners are compatible in this arena, they can draw courage from God to talk about and do something helpful in the other areas of intimacy.

TAKE ACTION

Now that we've talked about what a good marriage looks like, how do you rate your most important relationship? I hope you have lots of honest-to-intimacy A's on your marital report card. If you have mostly C's, D's and F's, then you are feeling trapped. It may feel like the death of a dream or your worst nightmare. A contrary point of view, however, might suggest this is the time of your greatest opportunity because you now are able to focus on the intimacy that needs the most help.

Here again, with God's help, you can choose your own actions. Will it be easy? Difficult? I don't know. I can't speak for you. I do know it will require a new way of thinking and behaving, as you restart your journey of growing closer together. It's my prayer that you are finding new hope for doing this in the book you are now reading. Up until now, you may have been passive, aggressive, perhaps both, which provides the ultimate confusion for your partner. Starting today, as you finish reading this chapter, you can choose to move from the darkness of confusion to the emotion of love. Could this really be the first and most exciting day of the rest of your married life? In your own heart you already know the answer. Running the risk of sounding like a tennis-shoe commercial, I encourage you to *just do it!*

7 -Trapped in Others' Expectations
. . . Up Until Now

What we allow, we teach.

Author Unknown

Some two thousand years ago, Aesop told this story:

One bright, sunny morning an old man and his grandson were going to market in a large town in the valley to sell a donkey. The donkey was beautifully groomed, brushed, and cleaned, and made to look attractive to any prospective buyer. Happily they set off down the steep path, leading the donkey. People they met along the way started making remarks about the old man and his grandson. "Look at that silly pair, scrambling and stumbling down that path when they could be riding comfortably on that donkey." So both of them got on the donkey.

They met another group who said, "Look at that lazy pair, breaking the back of that poor donkey." The old man, being heavier, got off and the boy continued to ride.

Further down the path they met others who said, "Look at that disrespectful child. He rides while the old man has to walk." So, the boy got off, and the old man rode.

"What a mean old man riding while that poor child walks," others complained.

By this time the man and boy were becoming increasingly bewildered. Finally, they met a group who criticized them for wearing out the donkey. A tired-looking donkey would be hard to sell.

After resting the donkey, they continued the journey. Thus, in late afternoon, gasping for breath, they entered the marketplace. Slung on a pole between them, tied by his feet, was the donkey.

The conclusion would appear to be this: If you try to please everyone, you will lose yourself.

Virtually every child, while growing

up, is taught to try to live up to the expectations of others, especially the adults around the child. Too often we bring this into adulthood as a kind of passive attitude that puts our own needs last and tries to keep everyone else happy. (Women are, either by nature or nurture, particularly adept at this.) But this kind of passivity can result in our simply moving from one trap to another, never able to pursue our own goals — or God's — or seek our own contentment.

The Real Meaning of Being Assertive

For me, walking the path of becoming assertive has been one of the most valuable experiences of my life. What is assertiveness? Let's take a thorough look at it. A long time ago a friend taught me to study by memorizing this old verse by Rudyard Kipling:

I keep six honest serving men
They taught me all I know;
Their names are what and where
And when and how, and why
    and who.

My friend explained that everything I had to study could be learned by using those six questions. So, let's use them now to examine assertiveness. *What* is assertiveness? It is when you take care of your own personal needs. This is not selfishness, because you are not getting your needs met at the expense of others. When we fail to get our needs met because we do not reveal our needs, we are in essence building a wall. We are separating ourselves from others. Far from making us more open, generous people, denying our own needs only makes us more selfish and grasping.

Who is the person with whom you must first be assertive? The answer is you. You are the only person you can change. Trying to change others is aggressive, controlling behavior. But changing yourself is appropriate behavior.

When can you change? Right now, of course. *Why* do you want to do all this? Because right now anger, fear and love are at war inside you, and that war can only bring pain. *Where* do you learn assertiveness? Right here, now. *How* do you become assertive? Read on.

Where Fear and Anger Meet

Assertiveness has two opposites: fear (or passivity) and anger (or aggression). To be fearful is to be passive, which means you keep your thoughts and feelings to yourself; you play it safe and you play it cool; you never let people know what you are feeling for fear you might upset them. The trouble with this approach is that you never get your own needs met, and you often end up trapped. Theology and psychology agree that we have not because we ask not. Bestselling author and communicator Father John Powell says, "When you build a wall, you must not only ask what am I walling out, but what am I walling in?"

Just as passivity builds walls and keeps us from relating to others, so does aggression. Losing your temper and shooting off your mouth, with little thought for others, is not an acceptable approach to building relationships. If anything, it sinks you deeper into a loveless, thankless existence where you remain trapped. The better news is that there is a healthy third alternative — loving assertiveness.

Let's say that last night you and your mate were discussing how stressed out you have been feeling. You are tired and out of sorts, you kick the dog, the kids are driving you nuts, you're eating too much, you have no balance in your life — all of which forces you finally to admit that you are trapped in an out-of-control spiral of emotional exhaustion. You need help and you want out! After taking a hard look at the demands you've been placing on yourselves, you and your spouse made the prayerful decision to slow down and adjust your schedules to carve out more time for yourselves and for your family.

We teach people how to treat us every day.

Okay, it's now ten o'clock the following morning and the phone rings. Your pastor is on the line, asking you to serve on another committee at church. He feels strongly that God wants you to do this job. In fact, *God told him to offer it to you!* Up until now, you would have put your own priorities aside and reluctantly said *yes* to your pastor when you heart wanted to say *no*. But then you would have been angry at yourself for caving in to his requests, and your mate would have been angry at you, too. It would have been a lose-lose situation.

Instead, you remember the decision you made only a few hours before. So this time you choose to assert yourself by saying, "Pastor, I understand how much you want me to be on this committee, and I appreciate your asking me. But my wife and I have looked at our schedules and our priorities, and I just don't have time." You didn't give the pastor a long list of *I'm sorrys,* unnecessary explanations, or Bible-verse-laden excuses why you chose not to participate. Nor were you worried about what the pastor might think of you because of your decision. You just said it! It felt good, for once, to take control of your life.

You were suddenly acting from your own God-directed control center, not reacting to the control of others. You were not passive, reacting out of fear; nor were you aggressive, responding in anger. You did not hurt your pastor with unkind, hostile words. You simply did what was right for you. You were *assertive:* acting in love, protecting your own rights, achieving your own goals, and feeling good about yourself in the process. You refused to be trapped. Congratulations. You are making remarkable progress.

Let's take a look at the diagram on the next page to see how this whole process works. There are three ways to respond to one's own needs: as a passive person, assertive person or aggressive person. These relate to the primary emotions of fear, love and anger. Do you want those results in your life? Are they traps you've fallen into? Have you been released by love, or do you still trap yourself through fear and anger?

Comparing Fear, Love and Anger

Fear	Love	Anger
Passive	Assertive	Aggressive
Submitting	Relating	Controlling
Has no rights	Protects own rights	Disregards rights of others
Fails to reach goals	Accomplishes goals,	Accomplishes goals at

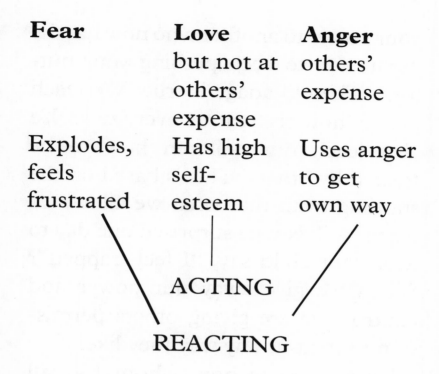

Fear	Love	Anger
	but not at others' expense	others' expense
Explodes, feels frustrated	Has high self-esteem	Uses anger to get own way

ACTING

REACTING

When you are relating to yourself or to someone else out of fear or anger, you are not relating at all. Fear keeps your feelings hidden; anger blows your feelings out. You are reacting. You don't have a relationship; you have a *reactionship*. You have abdicated your control. You have given your power to another who now has the permission to keep pushing your buttons. The old adage is true: We teach people how to treat us every day. We also teach our children how to be treated by others. This is based on the startling truth that what we allow, we teach. Will you be surprised one day to hear your child say, "I feel trapped"? When we give away our power and control, we are giving others permission to treat us any way they like.

I remember a boy (whom I'll call Johnny) sitting in my office, perched defiantly on his chair, arms crossed tightly across his chest, fists clenched as if he were riding a "white knuckler" at Disneyland. Trancelike, he glowers at his parents. His icy stares are weapons of aggression. But he is all visual. He has no ability to communicate his thoughts in a nonthreatening way.

I say to the young man, "Johnny, do you feel that because you have been free to live off your parents — without taking any responsibility or having any discipline in your life — that maybe their love for you has become a curse? Perhaps you don't know how to run your life *because your folks have run it for you for twenty-three years?*"

Bingo! He lights up, straightens up, gets up and speaks up. "Wow! I never knew it, but that's what I feel. That's why I'm so angry." Then he makes a most interesting statement. He says, "I wish they would have kicked me out when I was twenty-one and told me to get a job."

In therapy, it doesn't always happen so fast, but in those few moments that young man began the process of healing himself. And his parents began to face the fact that they could only be responsible for themselves, not for their son.

So, for them and for us, if we know and practice loving assertiveness, will we continue to be trapped in:

1. confused thinking?
2. a persistent past?
3. self-destructive fear?
4. seething anger?
5. compulsive sexuality?
6. a non-intimate marriage?
7. others' expectations?

I don't think so. We won't be trapped in these sticky areas any longer. Even if *up until now* we were.

TAKE ACTION

I encourage you to put assertiveness to work for you immediately. Start with the small daily demands put upon you, and work up to major areas where people and situations have kept you trapped in a confusing maze of purposeless activity or where you have failed to honestly tell others about your feelings and needs.

Submit or Defer?

Before we move on to the concluding chapter, I think we should tackle one of the more profound problems Christian couples continue to encounter. It relates to assertiveness and living up to others' expectations. It is being trapped in the misunderstanding of what God's Word teaches us in Ephesians chapter 5. In this Pauline letter, wives seem to be mandated by God to submit to and obey their husbands. (Or, in other interpretations, both husbands and wives are to submit to one another.) This is an unfortunate choice of words. Interestingly, scholars could have just as accurately gleaned from the text the word *defer*. How quickly this brings closure to the issue, because here, unlike with the word *obey,* we have a mutually warm feeling of love, compassion and understanding, all without doing damage to the original intent of God's Word.

Defer, according to *Webster,* means "to comply with the wishes, opinions or decisions of another." There is nothing harsh about deferring to someone else. Deference is kind and caring, and it seeks the best in another person. My wife Evelyn and I joke that we spend most of our lives trying to "out-defer" one another. It's a great problem to have, and one I wish for you and yours. In *The Message*, Eugene Peterson's version of the New Testament in contemporary idiom, this passage is translated as being "courteously reverent to one another." *To revere* means "to regard with great respect or devotion." Now we are into heart talk without the traps. How can traps exist when one is making attempts to out-defer the other? This is what the ultimate relationship between a man and a woman, according to the Bible, is all about.

8 -Trapped in a Loveless Existence

. . . Up Until Now

> The beauty of the world has two edges, one of laughter, one of anguish, cutting the heart asunder.
>
> Virginia Woolf

Their romance was like something out of a beautifully written love story. It was filled with the love, closeness and togetherness of a yearlong courtship. For once, Julie was truly in love. Just thinking about her beloved gave her the shivers. The two could not bear to be apart. Their hearts beat as one. Promises were made and kept; compassion was offered and delivered. Past challenges, broken friendships, and the chronic despair of another life were overshadowed by a new love, one that would *always* be there. A once-uncertain, even hostile, world had suddenly become warm, friendly, in sync with Julie's spirit.

Then, just as suddenly, there was a squealing of hot rubber, the screaming of bodies mangled and trapped in twisted steel, followed by a phone call from the authorities. In an instant, Julie's world was shattered. Everything she believed about her happiness turned cold and gray as the reality hit her: her best friend was gone from her earthly arms forever. She was trapped between a loving dream that died and a hideout nightmare that now invaded her mind. When she told me her story in my office a year later, she talked of not wanting to live. Though she told me suicide was out of the question, she later said there were times when it seemed to be a frightening option.

She left my office. A few hours later, as I was just closing up the center, she called and told me that a little sign on our elevator wall had gripped her heart. It said simply, *Spring Always Follows Winter*. It had prompted Julie to begin reflecting on the early days of her life where the snow would pile high and the temperature would drop to a freezing low each winter. Yet, she recalled, without fail, every year the snow and ice would melt, the warm sun would begin to shine, the green grass and fragrant flowers would return, and the birds would again reappear, bursting into song. It was true. Spring really *did* follow winter. She reminded herself there was no need to stay trapped in the snowdrifts of past problems, cold, isolated, frozen in anger and despair. All it took was a simple sign in our elevator to provide Julie with the gentle suggestion that things could change for her. And they did, in some remarkable ways, over the next year. She was able to break free.

Your Words Do Matter

Perhaps you are saying: "Good for her, but I live in a perpetual winter. Nobody cares about me or whether I live or die." Just maybe you do live in perpetual winter, and maybe there is no one who cares about you. But who is thinking this situation into existence? Who is saying, or at least implying, "I guess this is the way it is, and this is the way it will probably always be." Could it be the person reading this book? If so, I want you to take the risk of saying, "Up until now, this is the way it has been. But now I have a choice, and with a fresh spirit I will make today the first chapter of my new life filled with freedom and fulfillment." How can you say this? Because you now know that:

Freedom follows trappedness,
when creative love you choose.
For frustration, fear and anger
are all you have to lose.

That's why the words you use are

so vitally important. They tell the world who you are, what you are thinking, whether you see yourself as winning or losing, climbing or falling, victor or victim. The words you use bring you closer to others or push them further away. With that in mind, let's check out eight words that, whether you realize it or not, are actually shaping your life:

Did is a word of achievement.
Won't is a word of retreat.
Might is a word of deceiving.
Can't is a word of defeat.
Ought is a word of duty.
Try is a word each hour.
Will is a word of beauty.
Can is a word of power.

Empowered by Optimism

What words come out of your mouth day after day? Are you filling your life with expressions that demonstrate power and beauty, or is your world one that dwells on past efforts, helpless retreat, unkind deceit, self-deception, boring duty and noble attempts at action that never quite *do* anything significant?

TAKE ACTION

I want you to do a word inventory this week by keeping a journal of how you express yourself at home, at work, at church, at play. Pay attention to what you say and the emotion with which you say it. Ask yourself, *What can I learn from my speech, my attitude and how I come across to others?* The only real pain in your life comes from choosing to learn nothing from your actions. The pain of what's gone on before must push you to search for a new way. Your past no longer needs to be an obstacle to trap you; it can now be an opportunity for you to grow. This happens when you choose to "unlearn" your helplessness and pursue your hopefulness in God. Rather than feeling abandoned by God and others, as you've felt in the past, you now have the confidence to believe that you have a place of importance in your Father's world. Just as in the ancient story of the Prodigal Son, we modern addicts of pleasure who love running our own show can shout with joy that there is a way out if we go back to our Father's house.

> Becoming empowered by optimism in the "here and now" prevents you from becoming overpowered by pessimism in the "then and when."

You can, in fact, get out of your trap, whatever it may be. Perhaps you're even feeling like Nellie Forbush in the musical *South Pacific* as she sings of being a "cockeyed optimist" and being "stuck like a dope with a thing called hope." What a great thing to be stuck with! Hope. Hope for today and hope for your better future. With this growing optimism, you can now start appreciating yourself as you've never done before. The great word *appreciation* means "going up in value." Up until now, you have not thought so highly of yourself, but with God's help you have decided to grow into the person God designed you to be. You are no longer tearing yourself down; you are now taking the risk of building yourself up.

You are learning to live positively today with the negative voices of yesterday silenced. So what voices will you hear in your head at the dawning of each new day? What are your first feelings when you awaken from a night's sleep?

TAKE ACTION

You either choose to make your first thoughts of the day positive, or you choose to start out thinking negatively. Right away, in reading this, you might say, "But I'm just not a morning person. I always wake up feeling rotten." So this is the way you've been and will always be? Suppose I gave you one thousand dollars for every morning you started with ten minutes of positive thoughts? In a year, you would have three hundred and sixty-five thousand dollars, and you could get all the happiness that money will buy. But you really wouldn't need to because you'd already have happiness as the result of your new habit. Congratulations *morning person!* Isn't it fun to wake up feeling good?

Of course you don't want to become this new, vibrant, positive person all alone, but perhaps you are still fearful that you will have no one there to help you build yourself up. So let's learn how you can bring some appreciating ("going up in value") people into your life. You can do this with the clear determination to become the cause of your world and cease being a victim of someone else's world. You can now say, "I'm going to change from the fear that builds a wall to the faith that builds a bridge, and with God's help, I now take loving responsibility for, and control of, my life."

Up until now, the word *love* has not fit the context of your life. Now it will, because love looks for a way to be constructive. Think for a moment of the greatest love in your life. Do you remember how you felt valued and cared for? Loving words were followed by loving actions, which made you feel important to a special person. Psychologists and theologians agree that the greatest need of the human heart is to feel important to someone. When love builds you up, your response is, "I love you not only for what you are, but for what you are making of me." Think of someone looking deeply into your eyes and saying the words you just read. How does it feel? What's that you're saying? That it's never happened to you? I understand, but I also understand how you can make it happen. I think I can give you the insight you need right now to help you develop relationships that up until now you've been locked out of.

If you choose to believe and implement the following thought in your life, you will never be the same again: *Any loving thing you can dream about you can experience by doing it for someone else.* From now on you will think deeply about the implications of the Golden Rule. You've heard it all your life, but up until now you've not done much about it: Do to others what you would have them do to you. What would you like from a special person in your life? It may be a man or a woman. Let's say it's a man. You would like to be understood and cherished, in that order. This means that someone will become so deeply interested in you that he will want to draw you out with question after question so he can understand who you really are, perhaps even come to love you. He will seek to understand you before seeking to be understood by you. Will the cherishing follow immediately? Not quite yet. Now you give back to the person everything he gave to you. Right? But what if that person doesn't take the initiative? What if there are no questions asked? Then *you* must take the initiative, something you've never done, *up until now*. You take the initiative because you understand the truth that if the dream is to come true, it will start with you.

If the dream is to come true,
it will start with you.

If you want to break out of the trap of unloving relationships, hopelessness and despair, you must start reaching out to others as never before. You will be cherished only after you have been cherishing. It is *love's golden rule*.

To give love, though, you must first have it yourself. If it's going to be, it must start with He. He, in this theo-logically accurate but grammatically incorrect context, means God. We love him because he first loved us. This is more than a matter of words. It is the central part of history in which something extraordinary took place. It was the first historical event of a *giving* Christmas party. For God so loved the world that he gave his gift of love to your personal world. Having received this love, you can now experience living as a loved person.

When God is the central figure of your life, you receive the gift of God's power and insight for loving cre-atively. God alone is the Creator. But as a creator with a little *c*, you create the environment around you. Your thinking, translated into emotionalized actions, *sets up* or *sets off* the feelings of others. Your thoughts create truth in the minds of those who hear. You have the power to create truth because you have the loving Creator of truth.

Your love, your interest in others, gets through to people with life-changing messages. It draws from others the response you actively seek to create. So what do you most want to establish in a relationship? The word you might be seeking is *rapport*. This French word means "a harmonious, mutual understanding." It is an image of two people making beautiful music together, performing on their instruments with their well-trained skills. But what is most important is that *they are playing the same song at the same time!* They are creative artists. Perhaps this is why *The Art of Loving* by Erich Fromm is such a classic. Love, like music, is an art, not an accident.

The Fine Art of Listening
TAKE ACTION

How can you best begin reaching out to others to show them love? Perhaps you find it difficult to carry on a conversation with people you don't know well or with members of the opposite sex. You feel you might say the wrong thing, or you might have nothing to say at all, which would be even more terrifying! When you talk with someone on the phone, do *you* do most of the talking, which you fear, or most of the listening, which you can easily handle? If you're asking most of the questions and doing most of the listening, then you're getting on the wavelength of the other's feelings and opinions. You are getting to know and enjoy this person. So when the talk begins to run out, and you start to get a little scared, just say something you feel, such as "Gee, I enjoy talking with you." You say good-bye and hang up. How do you feel? Weren't you the one who fearfully told yourself that you can't carry on an interesting conversation? Up until now? Well, congratulations! You rose to the occasion and were an excellent communicator. It's quite possible that your friend had never heard someone tell her that *she was fun to talk to.* Perhaps you've never heard those words either. Up until now.

John Powell, in *The Secret of*

Staying in Love, puts it this way:

I want you to know that I do know what you need, even when I cannot give it to you. My own limitations and weakness will impede my performance, but I know that my greatest contribution to your life will be to help you love yourself. To think better and more gently of yourself. To accept your own limitations more peacefully in the perspective of your whole person. To give you all you need would require a wholeness in me that I do not have. I cannot come through for you always as you need me. But I can promise you this much. I will try. I will try always to reflect to you your unique and unrepeatable value and worth. I will try to be a mirror to your beauty and goodness. I will try to read your heart and not your lips. I will always try to understand you rather than judge you. I will never demand that you meet my expectations as the price of admission to my heart . . . so do not ask me why I love you. Such a question could invite only the response of conditional love. I do not love you because you look a certain way, or do certain things, or practice certain values. Only ask me this. Do you love me? And I can answer yes, oh, yes.

As we embody creative love, it becomes clear that love must be more than a sentimental expression of our feelings. Love is a *transitive verb,* which means that the act of love is an act that takes an object. Love has to be directed at someone or something. By directing your love at others, you change your world. Someone has said that the best way to predict your future is to create it yourself! Let's again explore how you can get out of the trap of old, useless models and start to create new behaviors in your relationships.

Two women in their early twenties moved from the Midwest and became part of a singles group in our California church. Six months after their arrival, they came together to see me for counseling. They seemed equally bright, and they were certainly attractive because they had wonderful, engaging personalities.

I asked, "How do you like the singles group at our church?"

One of them said, "It's okay, but I have a problem. Most of the men there just don't have it. Nine out of ten men are losers."

Now think about her comment for a moment. What does this say about her being passive or aggressive?

The other young woman said, "Gee, that's great!"

I was getting confused. "What do you mean, 'That's great'?" I asked.

The woman who had said this answered with a smile that encompassed her whole face. "Actually, it's very simple. If nine out of ten of the men are losers, then *one out of ten is a winner,* and I'm only looking for one."

Wow! What a great attitude. What a powerful example of being assertive. No traps for this woman. She knew what she wanted, and she was pursuing her dream without fear or anger. She was focused on her goal, and she planned to achieve it with a healthy attitude, along with large doses of good-natured humor. Within a year's time I married one of those women to an internist at a nearby hospital. The young doctor's wife had run away with another physician, and during his enormous pain, the emotionally shattered internist came to me to talk over his broken heart. I sent him off to our singles group where he met one of the two women who had come to me for counsel. Which one do you think he married? You know the one; it was the young woman who held a clear, uncluttered vision of her goal in her mind. The other woman is still trapped, still sees losers in her mind, and continues to react to her future more than act on it.

Searching for Something More

Throughout this book we have been looking at some new approaches — something more, something better — to help you see your world differently, creative ways to get you out of the traps of life that keep you in bondage. Let's look at this "something more" that has the explosive potential of making the rest of your life the best of your life. Up until now you have been perplexed, unsettled, trapped, trying to unravel the mystery of your own existence. Now, however, you have a renewed sense of control based on *God's love for you*.

TAKE ACTION

The question is, How will this work in your present relationships and in the new ones you will develop in the exciting days ahead?

First, the old control issues are gone. You don't have to be the boss anymore, nor will you ever again be trapped in reruns of the old temporary thrills of *instant physical binding* without the *loving bonding* of heart to heart.

How good it feels to know that with your new awareness there is something more than the trap of fighting for control. The power struggle is a thing of the past. No longer in the heat of an argument will you be arrogantly told, "The conversation is over," as though you've just been dismissed from an audience with your company boss! You finally know the *difference* and the *distance* between the *love of power* and the *power of love*. You have broken free, and you now choose to win love rather than win arguments, or lose them.

Love has the power to turn something less into something more.

You now understand that love has the power to turn something *less* into something *more*. As you become possessed by this love and acceptance of those around you, your love becomes contagious. Suddenly your "I really care for you" speaks volumes. The listener, though, might be asking, "Enough to be patient with me?" What do you say? As one who loves, you must indeed be patient with others as well as yourself. You may not have been patient, up until now, but now you no longer struggle for power, so patience becomes as natural as breathing. We are not advocating codependency here — taking care of someone who refuses to take care of himself or herself. There is a Grand Canyon of difference between patiently living to be responsible *for* someone and patiently loving when you are responsible *to* someone. That is no longer a trap for you because you are breaking free to honor others and help them become the people God designed them to be. When you break free, I mean *really* break free, then real life has finally begun . . . just as it did for this father.

A teacher in New York decided to

honor each of her seniors in high school by telling them the difference they each made. Using a process developed by Helice Bridges of Del Mar, California, she called each student to the front of the class, one at a time. First she told them how the student made a difference to her and the class. Then she presented each of them with a blue ribbon imprinted with gold letters that read, "Who I Am Makes a Difference."

Afterward the teacher decided to do a class project to see what kind of impact recognition would have on a community. She gave each of the students three more ribbons and instructed them to go out and spread this acknowledgment ceremony. Then they were to follow up on the results, see who honored whom and report back to the class in about a week.

One of the boys in the class went to a junior executive in a nearby company and honored him for helping him with his career planning. He gave him a blue ribbon and put it on his shirt. Then he gave him two extra ribbons, and said, "We're doing a class project on recognition, and we'd like you to go out, find somebody to honor, give them a blue ribbon, then give them the extra blue ribbon so they can acknowledge a third person to keep this acknowledgment ceremony going. Then please report back to me and tell me what happened."

Later that day the junior executive went in to see his boss, who had been noted, by the way, as being kind of a grouchy fellow. He sat his boss down and told him that he deeply admired him for being a creative genius. The boss seemed very surprised. The junior executive asked him if he would accept the gift of the blue ribbon and would he give him permission to put it on him. His surprised boss said, "Well, sure."

The junior executive took the blue ribbon and placed it right on his boss's jacket above his heart. As he gave him the last extra ribbon, he said, "Would you do me a favor? Would you take this extra ribbon and pass it on by honoring somebody else? The young boy who first gave me the ribbons is doing a project in school and we want to keep this recognition ceremony going and find out how it affects people."

That night the boss came home to his fourteen-year-old son and sat him down. He said, "The most incredible thing happened to me today. I was in my office and one of the junior executives came in and told me he admired me and gave me a blue ribbon for being a creative genius. Imagine. He thinks I'm a creative genius. Then he put this blue ribbon that says 'Who I Am Makes a Difference' on my jacket above my heart. He gave me an extra ribbon and asked me to find somebody else to honor. As I was driving home tonight, I started thinking about whom I would honor with this ribbon and I thought about you. I want to honor you.

"My days are really hectic and when I come home I don't pay a lot of attention to you. Sometimes I scream at you for not getting good enough grades in school and for your bedroom being a mess, but somehow tonight, I just wanted to sit here and, well, just let you know that you do make a difference to me. Besides your mother, you are the most important person in my life. You're a great kid and I love you!"

The startled boy started to sob and sob, and he couldn't stop crying. His whole body shook. He looked up at his father and said through his tears, "I was planning on committing suicide tomorrow, Dad, because I didn't think you loved me. Now I don't need to."

As we come to the last chapter in this book, the sun is rising in your life. Trapped feelings are dissipating. A new freedom is coming over you.

Breaking Free
. . . Trapped No More!

You must do the thing you think you cannot do.

> Eleanor Roosevelt

How do you break free when you are feeling trapped? What do you do to say good-bye to the pain of yesterday? How do you keep learning from the challenges of the past? How do you use your former bondage as a springboard to a life of renewed confidence, and then move ahead with greater understanding of yourself and others? How do you make the promise to

God and to yourself that you now believe in your heart that the truth has set you free? These are some of the questions we've been asking throughout these pages. What have been your answers, tentative though they may be? Have you been able to address the tough issues in your life where you once said "I can't" or even "I won't" and now add the phrase *up until now?* I hope that has been your choice.

Much of this book was written in my office at the Crystal Cathedral. On my wall was the mission statement of our counseling center, which read:

This ministry is a center for spiritual discovery and growth, where positive attitudes occur as a result of healed emotional and psychological hurts, where fragmented families are restored to wholeness, where bridges are built between emotionally distanced couples, and where individuals can blossom and grow in our "greenhouse," which is permeated with the love of Jesus Christ.

Since we cannot meet face-to-face, the next best thing is for me to bring the spirit of this ministry into your home by means of this book.

If it is to be, it's up to me is a slogan I've heard all my life, but the more I hear it and see it in action, the more I'm convinced it is true. These words, written on the tomb of an Anglican bishop in the crypts of Westminster Abbey in London, give credence to this slogan.

When I was young and free and my imagination had no limits, I dreamed of changing the world. As I grew older and wiser, I discovered the world would not change, so I shortened my sights somewhat and decided to change only my country. But it, too, seemed immovable.

As I grew into my twilight years, in one last desperate attempt, I settled for changing only my family, those closest to me, but alas, they would have none of it.

And now as I lie on my deathbed, I suddenly realize: *If I had only changed myself first,* then by example I would have changed my family.

From their inspiration and encouragement, I would then have

been able to better my country and, who knows, I may have even changed the world.

Too often we force the facts of life to fit our preconceptions, and when they don't fit, it seems easier to ignore them than to change our point of view. Up until now, one of those perceptions for you may have been, like the good bishop, that you planned to change the world. Unfortunately, personal growth doesn't work that way. For you to break free from the many traps we have discussed in chapters one through eight, the conversation must start with you. Mother Teresa reminded us in her profound simplicity that "to keep the lamp burning we have to keep putting oil in it." Only when you break free to become the person God created you to be, will you be able to provide the light of joy and happiness to those you love.

Only when you sit back and relax in the knowledge that "all things work together for good to those who love God" will you be comfortable enough to accept all the things that come your way. Of course, sometimes that "working together for good" is hard to see. Sometimes, like me, you want to say, "Hey, I loved God. But for the life of me I can't see the good in this, even though I can see my God."

Here's how my twenty-year-old daughter expressed the thoughts in her heart as she felt trapped in grief at the loss of her mother:

Lord . . .
You have someone very special to
    me
there by your throne.
She's the beautiful one
with the gentle eyes and the oh so
    kind
and loving words.
A special aura of quiet dignity and
    graciousness,
which we all so admired here on
    earth,
will truly make her stand out
    amongst
the other saints.

You know the one, Lord.
The saint who bypassed the pearly
    gates and
went straight to the choir room . . .

I find comfort in the completeness
    of your loving
control over our lives. But even
    your infinite peace
cannot remove the pangs of grief
    and sorrow
that pound at my heart
or the emptiness I feel without the
one who gave me life.

But, in your scheme of things,
thank you for also creating time
with its ability to gently, lovingly,
    ease the burden
of grief we feel.

Help me to see, Lord, as another
    has said,
"Beyond this world,
beyond myself,
Your sovereign plan

of seeing not,
may trust you."

You are still on the throne.
All is going according to plan . . .
Life does go on,
not *somehow,* but TRIUM-
PHANTLY.

Love, Carol

About the Author

Frank Freed, Ph.D., was the executive director of the Crystal Cathedral Counseling Center, having served in this position for many years. He is a graduate of Wheaton College, and holds graduate degrees from Stanford University, Fuller Theological Seminary and the Fuller School in Psychology. He has been licensed as a clinical psychologist by the California Medical Board since 1976. Dr. Freed also is an ordained minister in the conservative Baptist Church and served as a pastor for sixteen years.

The employees of Thorndike Press hope you have enjoyed this Large Print book. All our Thorndike and Wheeler Large Print titles are designed for easy reading, and all our books are made to last. Other Thorndike Press Large Print books are available at your library, through selected bookstores, or directly from us.

For information about titles, please call:
  (800) 223-1244
or visit our Web site at:
  www.gale.com/thorndike
  www.gale.com/wheeler

To share your comments, please write:

Publisher
Thorndike Press
295 Kennedy Memorial Drive
Waterville, ME   04901

Guideposts magazine and the *Daily Guideposts* annual devotional book are available in largeprint editions by contacting:
  Guideposts Customer Service
  39 Seminary Hill Road
  Carmel, NY 10512
or
  www. guideposts.org
or
  1-800-431-2344